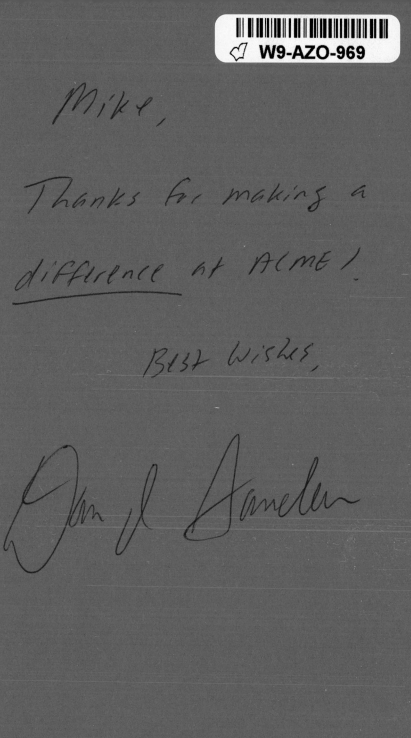

BUILT TO SERVE

*How to Drive the Bottom Line
with People-First Practices*

DAN J. SANDERS

New York Chicago San Francisco
Lisbon London Madrid Mexico City Milan
New Delhi San Juan Seoul Singapore
Sydney Toronto

1 2 3 4 5 6 7 8 9 0   DOC/DOC   0 9 8 7

ISBN-13: 978-0-07-149792-3
ISBN-10: 0-07-149792-7

This publication is designed to provide accurate and authoritative information in regard to the subject matter covered. It is sold with the understanding that neither the author nor the publisher is engaged in rendering legal, accounting, or other professional service. If legal advice or other expert assistance is required, the services of a competent professional person should be sought.

> —*From a Declaration of Principles jointly adopted*
> *by a Committee of the American Bar*
> *Association and a Committee of Publishers*

McGraw-Hill books are available at special quantity discounts to use as premiums and sales promotions, or for use in corporate training programs. For more information, please write to the Director of Special Sales, Professional Publishing, McGraw-Hill, Two Penn Plaza, New York, NY 10121-2298. Or contact your local bookstore.

Printed on acid-free paper.

For Neil,

Christian, entrepreneur, inventor, investor,
mechanical engineer, musician, outdoorsman,
philanthropist, photographer, pilot, and war veteran.
Husband, father, grandfather,
father-in-law and friend.

I miss you.

ACKNOWLEDGMENTS

B*uilt to Serve* is a labor of love, conceived on a golf course, nurtured and cared for in hotels across the country, and delivered to your bookstore thanks to the efforts of my friends and colleagues who served as temporary custodians along the way.

Special thanks to the entrepreneurial spirit embodied by the founder of United Supermarkets, H. D. Snell, Sr., and the living legacy of his family members, all of whom were incredibly supportive of this effort. Additionally, I am grateful to United's team members, whose lives reflect a humble desire to serve others, and to United's loyal guests, without whom there would be no story to write.

This book is a project of The Center for Corporate Culture, a platform dedicated to coaching leaders and their teams on the importance of culture as it relates to leadership, ethics, wellness, and execution in organizations. Much of the credit for *Built to Serve* belongs to The Center's co-founder, Claude Dollins.

I owe a great deal to Dan Dollins and all the members of The Dollins Group for their assistance in preparing the manuscript. Andy Hartman and Kathy Stringer, in particular, played key roles in assisting me with the creative and administrative challenges inherent in any project of this magnitude. Additional administrative help came from my research assistant, Andrea Heath; my personal assistant, Terry Rowland; and members of United's talent management team, Tom Weiss and Joni Andrews—all of whom made contributions that proved invaluable.

My dear friend Doug Hensley brought this manuscript to life through his timely editorial contributions, as did the staff in the McGraw-Hill Professional Trade group in New York, and Texas Tech University professors Robert and Marijane Wernsman. I am most appreciative of Mary Glenn's editorial input, personal encouragement, and professional commitment to publish *Built to Serve*.

Thanks to Dr. Stephen R. Covey, Ken Blanchard, and Dr. Kenneth Cooper for endorsing United's commitment to service before self and the principle-centered values embraced by United's leadership team.

I owe a debt of gratitude to many mentors, some of whom are mentioned here: Russell Anderson, Colonel Doug Cole, Brigadier General Edward (Buster) Ellis, Don Graf, Dr. Aubrey Green, Bill Henry, Major General Ken Hess, Robert Johnson, Harold Jones, Elaine Perrin, Dr. Ron Reed, Terry Sabom, Michael Starr, Dr. Barry Stephens, Steve Trafton, and Lieutenant Colonel Dick Wilson.

In addition, a special thanks to the mentors mentioned in this book: Dr. Leonard Berry, Dr. John Gourville, Larry Hays, Dr. L. Ken Jones, Lieutenant General Don Peterson, Galen Walters, Dr. E. Don Williams, and Colonel Forrest Whitlow.

While I was busy writing, several of our executive team members picked up the slack, and I am most grateful to each of them for their willingness to accept the extra load. Thanks to Gantt Bumstead, Matt Bumstead, Tony Crumpton, Sidney Hopper, Wes Jackson, Suz Ann Kirby, Michael Molina, Phil Pirkle, and Chris St. Clair.

I thankfully acknowledge my dear family, relatives, and friends for the wonderful blessing they represent in my life—especially my parents, L. J. and Virginia, and, of course, my wife, Shanna, our daughter, Shaley, and our son, Travis.

Most important, I thank God the Father, the creator of all things good, especially sustainable, culture-driven, people-centered organizations.

—Dan J. Sanders
Lubbock, Texas

CONTENTS

Contents

FOREWORD

I MEET FREQUENTLY WITH GROUPS of executives who express gratitude, even admiration, for the focus that we give to building principle-centered individuals, cultures, and institutions. But often they basically say this, "Wouldn't you agree that, at the end of the day, what really matters is profits or return on investment?" I immediately acknowledge the importance of the financial economics of an enterprise and suggest that it is primarily a by-product of what this book calls "higher math," that is, success in the marketplace, obviously, and success in the workplace (a sustainable culture-driven, people-centered organization).

I then try to teach the social ecology of how all of the elements are integrated and interdependent. The executives usually acknowledge the validity of what I am saying but emphasize the real end of what we're after (winning in the workplace and in the marketplace) has to do with winning for the owners. It's as if to say, "Yes, people are important, very important, but they are basically a means to an end—the end being profits." I often then counter with, "But if you see the people you're working with as partners, including your customers (which this book clearly teaches), would not the ultimate criterion by which everything will be evaluated by all stakeholders have to do with how well everyone's needs are really served?" It becomes impossible to separate these elements into independent entities or dimensions. It is clearly a social-ecological reality. The ultimate criterion that people use at the end of the day is how well all stakeholder needs are being served.

To paraphrase Arnold Toynbee, the great historian, you can summarize the history of all institutions, nations, as well as societies and civilizations in four simple words: "Nothing fails like success." In other words, if your response is equal to the challenge of today's reality, you'll have success. But if you're in a new challenge, the old successful response fails. That is essentially what is happening today. We're in a new reality, a new, global, digitized economy. The old industrial model of top-down command and control, even "kind" command and control, no longer works unless you are being subsidized or protected or unless the nature of your competition is local or regional and you're not really up against world-class competition, which the global economy is bringing us to more and more.

Summarizing Thomas Kuhn's landmark book called *The Structure of Scientific Revolution*s, every significant breakthrough throughout history is a break WITH. That is, a "break with" old ways of thinking, old ways of doing things, old skill sets, old tool sets. That is exactly what is happening in the world today as we move further into the Information/Knowledge Worker Age (which puts a premium on people, on their options and powers of choice, and on the kinds of interactions and communities they want to create). Even *Time* magazine put "YOU" as the person of the year for 2007, because of how the globalization of markets and technology has changed the name of the game in putting people at the center.

The real power of this marvelous book, in my judgment, lies in its spirit. If you're really open to it and let its compelling logic "have its way with you" for a period of time, it engages your spirit. It captures your spirit. It *inspires* your spirit. You come to realize that in the last analysis, we are "built to serve." Our happiness, our fulfillment, that which gives our life meaning, purpose, and direction, come from service. This means serving all the people around us, including, in business, our primary business partners: customers, suppliers, associates, owners, managers, and so forth. The first time I read this book, I was riveted by the spirit of the idea that serving is the purpose of life and by how an organization and its culture, animated by this higher math, can alone make it sustainable.

Dan Sanders shares so many of his experiences in business, in sports, and in life, to powerfully communicate the values of friendship, servanthood, integrity, and excellence, all buttressed by humility, which I believe is the mother of all virtues (courage being the father and integrity the child).

In the book, the word "culture" is used a lot—sustainable, culture-driven, people-centered organizations. Isn't that an interesting expression? Culture driven? What does that mean?

The great sociologist Émile Durkheim taught, "When mores are sufficient, laws are unnecessary. When mores are insufficient, laws are unenforceable." Mores are the norms, the values of a group of people. As we move out of the Industrial Age, top-down, carrot-and-stick motivated organization into the new Knowledge Worker economy, we create a culture and community of people who share a common vision and set of values that serve as guidelines in all decision making and that make everyone accountable to everyone else. In short, culture driven. Gone are the days when the person at the top takes responsibility to establish the vision and communicate the values and then continuously "communicate, communicate," "sell, sell," "incentivize, incentivize" around that vision and set of values. Instead, this vision, this purpose, this mission, these values, become impregnated into the very soul of the community, of the entire culture. Everyone feels accountable to them and accountable to each other, and also enthused and excited by them. They feel it in their bones. It's not something that is handed down from above. It is part of the social ecology. Everyone possesses this value system and common belief about working toward a shared vision and mission to serve, and they treat each other based upon the natural laws or principles that create sustainability. Leadership then becomes shared and is part of the culture. Different people serve different needs in different ways because of their unique talents and gifts and strengths. Ultimately you reach a point where you have a blended social ecology, a culture of complementary teams whose strengths are made productive and whose weaknesses become irrelevant through the strengths of others, a culture that respects the importance and role of every person and flattens the organization. Leadership then becomes more a *choice* than a *position*. Moral authority rather than formal authority alone.

Those who live on yesterday's achievements but add no new value today, those who violate universal, timeless principles such as deceiving customers or mistreating subordinates, those who constantly borrow strength from their position or formal authority to get things done will find their lives are in violation of the culture, and most will, in their discomfort, select themselves out and go elsewhere.

This is not just a theoretical treatise and a well-thought-through message on being built to serve. It comes from the heart and soul of people who have done it. It's the United Supermarkets' model, taught in a most excellent and successful way, even though they'll be the first to admit they are far from perfect.

Very few people understand the concept of culture. They think it's something that is produced through leadership, through effective communications, through inspiring, visionary statements. Even though these are important elements, the real heart and soul of a culture emerges as paradigms (beliefs as to how the world works) combined with principle-based values that people come to respect, to believe in, to live by, and to hold each other accountable to.

Sincere, open-minded readers of this book will love it because it is eminently practical, with numerous illustrations that you will identify with. Its logic is compelling, and the social-ecological paradigm is beautifully taught and illustrated. But above all, it is the spirit of the book that touches your spirit. Our true DNA is that we are built to serve. The cultural DNA which overlays this true DNA teaches us that the greatest are those who are being served and, therefore, profit and position and power and prestige become the key elements and definitions of success. The spirit and content of this book penetrate through that cultural DNA and reawaken our true DNA, our true nature, and enliven our conscience, our inward sense of what is right and what is wrong, and energize our desire to make a difference, to really contribute, to add value—in short, to serve.

The true identity theft is not financial; it is spiritual. People are nourished by a selfish culture toward "what's in it for me." They have lost their true self. As one put it, "when man found the mirror, he began to

lose his soul." The point is, he became more concerned with his image than with himself.

This book helps to restore our true self. We were
built to serve.

—STEPHEN R. COVEY

PREFACE

W HAT YOU ARE ABOUT to read is a story of experiential discovery. From growing up around an authentic cowboy on a West Texas ranch to piloting a high-performance jet to altitudes above 70,000 feet, it is an account that reveals a valuable lesson regarding leadership: culture and people, not Wall Street and investors, create sustainability.

The stories in *Built to Serve* remind us that seeking a higher purpose ultimately leads to personal growth, professional fulfillment, and success in life. Many of the stories are of familiar events, organizations, or institutions—Southwest Airlines, NASA, Air Force One, and Watergate. But some of the names may be less familiar. For example, names like Lubbock Christian University, Gallery Furniture, and adplex are likely to be new to the reader. Their stories will pique your interest and create a desire to learn more about the cultures and people that differentiate them from other organizations.

United Supermarkets is a company not widely known, but its story—the story I tell as the person fortunate enough to serve as its CEO—is central to *Built to Serve*. Founded in 1916 by H. D. Snell, Sr., the son of an Oklahoma cotton farmer, United has quietly become one of America's oldest family-owned corporations. Snell did not have a degree from Harvard, Yale, or Princeton. In fact, he never earned a college degree, yet through hard work and extraordinary perseverance, he created a splendid legacy built on the contributions of ordinary people. Today, nearly 75 grocery stores throughout Oklahoma and Texas owe their success to Snell and his descendants.

In the supermarket industry, where size is a popular strategy, United manages not just to survive, but to thrive. One reason for its success is that United's team members are genuinely considered family, and United's workforce displays the rhythm and innovation of a seasoned team.

The family's vision is synonymous with its ministry—serving people and enriching the lives of others. The company's mission is defined by just six words: Ultimate Service, Superior Performance, and Positive

Impact. United is a well-known and well-respected member of the communities it calls home, and its stores serve more than one million guests each week. For some guests, the journey is familiar—one their parents, their grandparents, and their great-grandparents made. For others, it is a new and refreshing approach to shopping for food and related products. Regardless, the result is the same—raving fans and loyal shoppers.

What makes the experience so unforgettable? While most companies these days rely on cutting costs to survive, we are sustained by a culture-driven, people-centered approach to business. As Matt Bumstead, co-president and great-grandson of the company's founder, puts it, "Our family takes how people are treated personally." From the newest recruit to the team's veteran players, our people connect what they do to who they are in a manner that has earned them national recognition. Our team members recognize personal relationships are their business—the fact that they sell bananas, bread, and milk is seen as incidental.

Additionally, United has established itself as a philanthropic entity that models the best of solid corporate citizenry in the communities where it has planted stores. In fact, United's team members once donated

$10 million to Texas Tech University to help fund a 15,000-seat, on-campus, all-purpose facility, which is known as United Spirit Arena. Despite the gift's high-profile nature, United's leaders prefer to operate without fanfare—just the way the founder would have wanted it.

I have been privileged to be part of this remarkable journey. I trust you will find the journey as rewarding to read as it has been to experience.

INTRODUCTION

The Southwest Airlines 737 we were aboard had just leveled off at 35,000 feet en route to California when I knew something was wrong. For a moment, I tried to pretend it was not happening. I forced myself to think about other things—the golf my son and I would play at Pebble Beach, the trip down to Carmel for shopping, and the view of the ocean from The Lodge. I was jolted by what was happening, and I soon found myself in a heavy sweat.

The nausea came fast. My vision blurred. The flight attendant near the back of the plane saw what was happening and rushed to help. By the time she reached me, I was no longer conscious. A paramedic traveling with his new bride on their honeymoon immediately began treating me, and he was soon joined by another passenger, a doctor from Amarillo, Texas. Working together, they resuscitated me and stabilized my body while the jet began its descent into El Paso, where I was taken by ambulance to Del Sol Hospital for what became a one-week stay.

In the following weeks, every flight attendant who had been aboard the jet that day called to check on my condition. Most of them took the time to write a note. Several months after the ordeal, the airline's management team was still corresponding with my family—the airline even sent free travel coupons to the off-duty paramedic and the vacationing physician who had helped stabilize me. Not surprisingly, I became a champion for Southwest, telling my story to anyone who was interested. Southwest Airlines knows what most organizations have either forgotten or never understood: there is something special about being built to serve others.

T HE GLOBAL BUSINESS CULTURE that prevails today is broken. What is needed is a radical transformation—a monumental paradigm shift that will reshape our present understanding of the true purpose of work. Such a change requires great courage and a compelling sense of urgency, but a proven formula exists. It begins with accepting the idea that an organization's culture is the wellspring of sustained success.

When the culture models this kind of vibrancy, such positive elements as growth, profitability, and good corporate citizenry are natural by-products. People are fulfilled professionally and personally, and organizations find deep meaning, resulting in a positive impact on the communities they serve. This is a business model that places people ahead of profits and service ahead of statistics.

Any organization requires technical competence, but that quality by itself will not allow an enterprise to realize its full potential. In truth, sustainable organizations have leaders who model a service-oriented culture that holds human beings in high regard and seeks opportunities to make a positive impact for all stakeholders.

Sustainability is a key concept to grasp because it establishes a context for decision making within an organization. Think about it from a personal perspective. When we make choices regarding what activities we pursue and what foods we eat, do we give any consideration to the long-term positive or negative effects of our decisions? We should. Such decisions have a great deal to do with our ability to maintain or prolong our existence on this planet. Most, if not all, of the choices we make as human beings should be made with a desire to live long, active lives followed by exceedingly short deaths.

Likewise, sustainable organizations also focus on the longer view. They operate in a manner aimed at maximizing their time on the planet and giving them long, active lives. Decision making in this context is healthy, characterized as nurturing and supportive. Regrettably, however, a large percentage of organizations today are created not to serve, but to sell. They pursue a short-term agenda, resulting in decision making that is myopic, exploitative, and destructive. Typically, such organizations place a low priority on people and seek to satisfy only a limited number of stakeholders.

Sustainability, then, is really a process of balancing the short-term needs of an organization's people with the long-term needs of the organization's purpose. The process requires committed leadership, but for those leaders who are willing to accept the challenge, the result is a competitive edge that ensures prolonged success for their organizations.

Such is the case with Southwest Airlines. In an industry plagued by economic turmoil, no other airline can match Southwest's sustained success. Texans are well acquainted with Southwest's commitment to excellence as well as its ability to defy conventional thinking in the industry. While other airlines are scrambling for answers, Southwest flies above the turbulence. What sets this organization apart? Simply put, it is the people and the culture, in that order.

Management at Southwest Airlines knows other companies will attempt to copy everything the company does, but they also know culture is not something built from the outside in.

A sustainable culture is built from the inside out. It starts with leadership that places the highest level of importance on human beings and a corresponding premium on recruiting, hiring, and training—both academic and experiential training—to equip and empower them.

People are acknowledged as the organization's greatest assets, not mere expenses relegated to a line on a profit-and-loss statement. In fact, when I became a military pilot, one of the first things I learned was never to refer to my cargo as "passengers." Instead, I was taught to refer to people as "souls on board." While this might seem a minor choice of words, it communicated volumes to me regarding the value of each person and the importance of maintaining safety in flight. The same must be said about organizations.

Great cultures transcend industry segments and promote universal truths. My friend and mentor Dr. Stephen Covey has spent much of his life teaching and reminding leaders and followers alike that natural principles endure over time. His years of research support the idea that culture is not just important to an organization—it is everything to an organization. Dr. Covey takes this a step further, connecting the role of personal faith to organizational principles.

I was seated next to him at an Ethical Leadership Conference in the fall of 2006. Our conversation turned to the topic of culture and its importance in the workplace. I asked Dr. Covey what he thought about my company's practice of praying before meetings and before making important decisions. In the private sector, it is lawful for an employer to incorporate prayer in meetings, whatever the prevailing beliefs. However, my question was prompted by warnings from attorneys that open expressions of faith in the workplace are sometimes problematic.

Dr. Covey's answer was simple and direct. "The next time anyone warns you of what might happen if you continue to pray before meetings and important decisions," he said, "tell them you're more concerned about what might happen if you don't."

It was a great answer, and one I wish I had thought of first, especially given my own commitment to godly values. *A people-centered culture does not compromise values; rather, it seeks to remain faithful to values—even when remaining faithful means doing things differently from everyone else.* Remember, a legendary culture is created in the head and the heart of the leader and passed from team member to team member.

This is certainly the case with United Supermarkets. Like Southwest Airlines, United enjoys a legendary culture that sustains its ability to compete in an industry that has been turned upside down by commodity pricing, a cluttered marketplace, and razor-thin profit margins. Founded in 1916 by H. D. Snell, Sr., United celebrated its ninetieth year of continuous service in 2006.

One family owns this regional chain. Its primary competitor, Wal-Mart, is more than 300 times its size. The chain also competes with large consolidators in the industry, such as Safeway and Kroger. Even so, United quietly records increases in sales and total customers (called "guests" at United) decade after decade.

Why? Fueled by the crucial contributions of thousands of team members, United's culture sets the company apart from its peers, large and small. Yet the company does not rely on training manuals or checklists to serve as shortcuts that team members can use in determining how to conduct business. Instead, the company depends on a nine-decade track record of success modeled by leaders and embraced by new hires to create walking, talking ambassadors of its culture.

A leader's actions, not words, form the basis for learning and eventually handing down a culture. Nowhere is this more prevalent than in the armed forces. I served as an Air Force officer and pilot for more than a decade, and I came to treasure the military culture. Contrary to the often-maligned image of military life, my experience was extraordinary. Of course, as one might expect, flying high-tech jet aircraft was as rewarding as it was challenging, but the enduring fulfillment of the job came from the deep meaning of the mission. I think this can be said of all military endeavors.

Clearly, money is not the primary motivator for military service. My hazardous duty pay amounted to about $110 per month. Of far greater value was the small ribbon or tiny medal awarded to me in recognition of my sacrifice. The next time you see a member of the military in uniform, note the ribbons or medals. They speak volumes. Decorating service members regularly is an important part of the military's culture.

United is a huge believer in the importance of recognition programs. We have a standing policy that when leaders are not involved in a specific task, they are expected to write a personal note, send an e-card, or engage in a personal conversation to acknowledge the contribution of a team member.

I am regularly surprised by the number of people who come up to me and make a reference to a personal note I wrote them two or three years earlier. Team members remember when leaders make the time to take the time.

In my lifetime, I have had the good fortune of living and working in and around organizations where culture mattered. Long before my first professional endeavor, my family's culture of love and support proved a wonderful blessing. Essentially, all the elements of a great childhood and upbringing surrounded me.

One of the blessings I enjoyed most was the opportunity to get to know my grandparents. My maternal grandparents lived in Plains, Texas. My grandfather,

H. B. Price, was a true cowboy—a successful rancher, a man's man in every sense of the word. He rolled his own cigarettes, wore a sweat-stained gray Stetson, and spent most of his life in the saddle. My grandmother was the consummate country cook who devoted her life to preparing meals in the kitchen. For a young boy raised in the city, trips to the ranch were adventurous, educational, and fulfilling. As a rule, people working on a ranch or farm acquire a lot of wisdom; my grandfather was no exception.

Among his most enduring life lessons was one regarding the manner in which we as human beings approach work. As on any working ranch, there was always plenty of work to go around, and a "vacation" on the ranch was code talk for work that needed to be done. I visited the ranch one summer at a time when the garden, which was just behind the ranch house, required tending.

My grandfather escorted me to the garden one afternoon and said, "You need to pick up all of these small rocks." It was hot and windy, and I imagined a hundred other things I would rather be doing. Even so, I grabbed an old tin bucket and began picking up rocks. After what seemed like a long time, I became uninterested, tired, and unproductive.

I had reached the point where I was sitting on the bucket instead of putting rocks in it when my grandfather saw me from a distance and made his way to the garden gate. "You're not making much progress, sonny boy," he said. He was right. I had barely made a dent in the number of rocks in the garden. I responded truthfully, "I'm bored, and I don't like picking up rocks."

Then something special happened.

He said, "Let me ask you a few questions. What do you like?"

"Sports," I said.

He continued, "Do you like basketball?"

I perked up. "I love basketball!"

He said, "Let me ask you something. This bucket you have here is about the same size as a basketball hoop, right?"

"Yes, sir," I answered.

"What if this bucket was a basketball hoop and these rocks were basketballs. How many baskets do you think you could make in thirty minutes?"

I picked up a small rock and executed a little jump shot, and the rock landed in the center of the bucket. "Whoosh," I exclaimed.

Then he said, "Can you do a hook shot?"

I picked up another rock and did a little hook shot, and that rock went into the bucket, too.

Then he said, "Well, how many of those can you do in a row?"

As daytime became nighttime, the rocks disappeared one by one, and my imaginary basketball game kept me thoroughly entertained.

It was a lesson worthy of an Ivy League diploma—a glimpse into the way people are wired. I have often reflected on this lesson while educating corporate leaders on the difference between advertising and marketing. When my grandfather told me rocks needed to be picked up in the garden, he was simply *advertising* the fact we had rocks in the garden.

However, when he convinced me the bucket was a basketball hoop and the rocks were basketballs, he was *marketing* something different. Once I made his perspective on the job my own, I enjoyed getting the job done because the garden of rocks was now the basketball court at Madison Square Garden, and I was the star forward of the New York Knicks. What seemed torturous, frustrating, and discouraging actually turned out to be a highlight of my summer's stay. People-centered cultures are focused on *marketing* the work, not on *advertising* work that needs to be done.

We all know unglamorous jobs exist in any profession. Even so, the successful completion of the work is largely the result of our mental approach to the task. *Cultures focused on people unleash the imagination and lift performance to new heights—to a higher purpose.* Max De Pree, the gifted CEO emeritus of Herman Miller, put it this way: "The future can be created, not simply experienced or endured." In the right kind of culture, De Pree's statement is true.

Therefore, this is a book about changing the future of organizations and the people they serve. I believe God created human beings to serve, and since organizations are composed of human beings, they should be service-oriented. When you create an enterprise to serve others' needs first (the equivalent of subscribing to a higher purpose), great things happen for all involved.

Contrary to popular belief, organizations can have a culture-driven, people-centered philosophy and still deliver superior performance. Consider this: an investment in creating the right kind of culture delivers big returns. A study conducted by Deloitte Consulting tracked the shareholder returns of the 56 publicly traded firms on *Fortune* magazine's 100 Best Companies to Work For list in 2006. The facts revealed that those firms consistently outperformed the S&P 500. Genentech, one of America's best-known biotech firms and number one on *Fortune*'s 2006 list of the 100 Best Companies to Work For, understands the concept of directing and focusing energy on employees and customers while still providing an exceptional return to shareholders.

Businesses today focus an enormous amount of time on financial performance but appear to be indifferent to the way employees are valued and treated. We pore over profit-and-loss statements and obsess over quarterly financial reports, which prompt a litany of questions regarding past activities. We analyze financial statements formatted to suit a nineteenth-century manufacturing plant—statements that neatly categorize me as an expense of the business, but the computer I am working on as an asset of the business. It is time to change.

The most important questions should be those that ascertain the organization's potential and assess how best to unleash the power of the workforce. One reason for our fixation on past performance is that it is easier to see where you have been than to accurately predict where you are going. *To predict the future, you need to understand an organization's potential, which requires knowing how to maximize the talents of the people you employ. This is where culture matters most.*

An organization will never fully realize its potential if it does not engage its people in a higher purpose.

All too often, business leaders continue to have a misguided perception that suggests the real purpose for their organization's existence is profit, and the things that matter most are power, position, and money. Nothing could be farther from the truth for an organization seeking sustainable success. A compelling option worthy of consideration centers on nurturing people to render ultimate service.

Failure to act on this reality may leave companies with a crippling labor drain as a result of the globalization of the labor market. In addition, virtually all products and services without compelling differentiation are or will eventually be commodity-priced. An organization's ability to serve will be the last tool that can provide a competitive advantage in a crowded marketplace. Organizations desiring sustained success simply must embrace a culture-driven, people-centered philosophy.

Consider this: in virtually any supermarket in America today, you can purchase a pound of bananas grown thousands of miles from the store; transported to a regional distribution center within days of harvest; ripened in a multimillion-dollar, climate-controlled chamber until they are ready for consumption; retransported to individual stores; stocked by employees; and sold for about 25 cents. No wonder the supermarket industry understands what it means to succeed on less than 1 percent of net income.

Companies counting on gross profit margins significantly increasing in the future will fail. Only those companies that price their goods and services as inexpensively as possible will thrive, especially for items that have no differentiation from the competition. The relentless pressure for cheaper product pricing that is applied to organizations today has expedited the globalization of labor, forced the issue of outsourcing, and destroyed otherwise healthy corporate cultures. Once this happens, organizations become vulnerable to any competitor that brings a lower price to the market. No loyalty exists when the nature of the relationship between the buyer and the seller is based on price and nothing more.

So what can you do to ensure your organization focuses on culture and people? How will a culture-driven, people-centered environment create fulfillment and meaning for all stakeholders? What benefits can be realized by seeking a higher purpose? This book will answer these questions.

PART ONE

BUILDING
A PEOPLE CULTURE
IN A NUMBERS
WORLD

UNDERSTANDING HIGHER MATH

Medtronic is a leader in medical technology. However, it is so much more. The company provides lifelong solutions for patients with chronic pain, and it also manufactures prosthetic valves for use in hearts. Each day, Medtronic employees take their places on a sophisticated line of production and assembling stations and produce cutting-edge components to precise specifications.

The shifts are long. The work is tedious. There is no room for error. Yet Medtronic retains employees at a remarkable rate while maintaining high morale in its workforce. Recently, United retained Dr. Scott Cawood, a business consultant with ModernThink Consulting, who knows how a company's culture *correlates with its success over the long term because he has spent years analyzing companies with service-oriented cultures. Cawood shared his knowledge of Medtronic during a strategic session with our executive team in which we examined best practices.*

Dr. Cawood told us that he had spent a lot of time talking to Medtronic's rank-and-file employees, and that those conversations had revealed a powerful conclusion: Medtronic's employees had their own perceptions of their contributions to the company. They did not see themselves as producing heart valves. They unwaveringly believed they were saving lives.

20

In a tangible stroke of brilliance, Medtronic capitalized on that perception, creating an annual event where employees could meet patients who were alive because of transplanted artificial hearts containing Medtronic technology. That realization allowed Medtronic to provide a context of higher purpose for its workforce, resulting in focused and fulfilled employees.

Mᴇᴅᴛʀᴏɴɪᴄ ɪs ᴀᴍᴏɴɢ ᴀ ᴍɪɴᴏʀɪᴛʏ of organizations in its commitment to a people-centered culture. The majority of organizations continue to embrace power and money as the only real measures of success. It is true: power and money appear to be the ultimate rewards, according to today's culture, despite history's repeatedly teaching otherwise. Popular corporate culture tells us that more is better, but those who appear to have it all often really have the least. They are unaware, unhappy, and unfulfilled.

Patrick Morley, author of *The Seven Seasons of a Man's Life*, suggests that poor people may be the luckiest people of all because at least they have the hope that if they had money, they would be happier. I have found the truth is just the opposite—power and money will never satisfy the soul.

Organizations that make people and service the cornerstones of their corporate identity enjoy sustainability. The misguided and myopic notion that places a premium on power and money has no permanence in today's marketplace.

Mired in egomania and denial, business continues to sink into a morass and worship these false idols of power and money. The stories documenting titans of industry that became colossal failures as a result of selfishness and outright greed seem almost commonplace today. Adelphia, Arthur Andersen, Enron, L&H, Tyco, and WorldCom are just a few of the more

21

prominent companies implicated in such behavior since 2000.

Regrettably, a significant number of companies today are eating away at their business culture and destroying the lives of honest, hardworking people. When businesses come to be dominated by numbers at the expense of people, they forget their real purpose and focus more on populating spreadsheets than on enriching lives.

I experienced this firsthand as an executive in 2002, when we sold a majority ownership of our company to a group of financial investors. The transaction certainly appeared to be a positive move for our team members at the outset; however, we soon realized that there would be a significant change in the way the company's business was expected to be conducted.

For example, we closed the transaction in New York City on a Friday and enjoyed a brief weekend celebration. At 7 a.m. Monday, I arrived at the office in Houston to find the phone already ringing.

It was a financial analyst associated with the firm that had purchased our company. He said, "Hey, Dan, what are you doing?"

I told him I had just arrived in the office and had not even turned my computer on. He told me he needed some information for a presentation by noon.

He said, "Here's what I need. I'm filling out a spreadsheet, and I need your projected sales, by customer and by product, for the years 2003, 2004, 2005, 2006, and 2007."

I heard him ask the question, but I thought he was joking. I explained to the young analyst that there was no way I could possibly know what product was going to sell three years from now or what client would purchase that product three years from now. I told him that any such number would be meaningless.

His response was, "Look, I need a number for my spreadsheet."

I reiterated the number would be nothing more than a wild guess. He said he did not care whether it was a guess or not. He needed a number.

It dawned on me that day: it was not even 8 a.m., and something terrible had happened. The majority owner was no longer motivated by a desire to help team members and clients realize their potential.

In 48 hours, the conversation had turned from meaningful relationships to meaningless numbers.

It is precisely this philosophy that has created the many documented failures in corporate America—the staggering number of organizations that fail within ten years of their initial opening. However, the sobering truth is beginning to bring about positive changes. Some organizations are responding favorably, embracing new ideas, and adopting timeless universal truths.

Even so, business culture is at a crossroads. Changing it involves choice. It also will involve courage on the part of those organizations facing the challenge of taking steps to reverse the trend.

Too many organizations today are tangled in a web of "financial adultery"; on the one hand, they are engaged in a love affair with spreadsheets, numbers, and the pursuit of wealth, while on the other hand, they are obligated to the welfare of the human beings who generate those numbers. Now mix in financial experts from corner offices thousands of miles away in some instances, and this form of cheating seems innocuous.

Sadly, in this popular business model, an organization's workforce is expected to keep churning out profits in a manner not too dissimilar to the machines that fueled the Industrial Revolution.

If you subscribe exclusively to the belief that everything has to have an immediate return on investment, you will never fully comprehend higher math. It requires an equal commitment to such things as safety, training, loss prevention, wellness, and benefits, the so-called soft matters that are essential to sustainability but rarely create a short-term return on investment.

Amid the complexity of these trends, a fable comes to mind—one we learned as children: "The Goose That Laid the Golden Eggs."

A man and his wife had the good fortune to possess a goose that laid a golden egg each day. Despite the fact that fate had smiled on them, it wasn't long before their greed took control. Imagining that the bird's insides must be made of gold, they decided to kill the goose to build their fortune at once. Upon the bird's death, they found that it was like any other goose. Thus, they neither got rich all at once, as they had hoped, nor enjoyed the daily addition to their wealth any longer.

25

Understanding this fable is critical to grasping higher math. It involves a conscious choice: either you pay attention to the people producing the results or you never realize their maximum potential. Too often, detached business leaders concentrate on what is next rather than proactively attacking what is now. The inescapable reality is that the human factor ensures sustainability in a culture-driven, people-centered organization, and savvy leaders acknowledge this.

Higher math, then, requires an emotional alignment of the leader with all levels of the workforce. It is a matter of escaping the mahogany foxhole and avoiding leadership in a vacuum. It is about building trust and having a positive impact on people. A friend put it this way: "You must surrender the armor of indifference."

Financial statements are only a small part of the story. Spreadsheets fail to convey the emotional status of an organization's leadership. They are tools and nothing more—fine when it comes to numbers, of limited use when it comes to the human factor.

Consider this example. At United, we regularly remind team members of the difference between a storekeeper and a merchant. Storekeepers are custodial in their approach to business. They get up each morning, unlock the store, turn on the lights, and ensure that team members are in place and product is on the shelves in accordance with the corporate plan.

Once those tasks are completed, they wait for guests to show up and buy something. At the end of the day, they collect sales figures and send them to the home office, where the accounting staff fills out financial reports, which, in turn, the executives review. As elementary as it sounds, this is precisely the model used by many businesses today—and to the extent the basic math adds up, it works fine.

Now, in the spirit of understanding higher math, contrast the storekeeper with the merchant. Merchants are entrepreneurial. They complete the same tasks as storekeepers in getting the store ready for business, but they take extra time to personally engage each team member and thank that team member for what they hope will be a stellar contribution that day.

Financially, merchants approach the day as if the cash registers are empty, and it is the team's mission to fill them. They think of the money as their own, not the corporation's. They will take the risk of deviating from the corporate plan because they have confidence in the idea that the company's higher purpose is people, not just profit.

At day's end, the home office gets the figures in the same way that it gets the storekeeper's figures. However, the merchant's figures reflect a radically different level of engagement. The storekeeper wants to maintain the status quo, but the merchant is never content with today's performance because tomorrow represents an opportunity for improvement. To the man-

27

agers sitting in the corner office thousands of miles away, the figures fit nicely on the same spreadsheet, but they tell significantly different stories.

Inherent in this storekeeper-merchant comparison is the belief that an organization's potential is important. *People-centered organizations speak the language of potential—not so much as it relates to a sales number, as important as that may be, but rather as it relates to the workforce itself.*

Simply put, engaging people in a manner meant to maximize their contributions makes a difference for both the organization and its people.

My father was a petroleum engineer. During his 35-year career, he took on many challenges, but perhaps none more rewarding than the Bravo Dome project in the oil-rich Permian Basin of West Texas. This innovative undertaking involved injecting carbon dioxide into wells to enhance production.

Introduced 25 years ago, this technology is still in use today as a means of maximizing oil recovery. Similarly, people-centered organizations take an innovative approach to injecting people with spirit-lifting energy to reach new levels of performance. Cultures able to create this advantage achieve sustainable success.

It seems odd the business culture struggles with the concept of a genuine focus on the uniqueness of employees, especially given the concentrated effort made to connect with customers. Without an emotional investment in team members, there will be an emotional void in the effort to sustain customers.

From a branding perspective, it is easy to accept the idea that the best brands generate an emotional connection with customers, but that cannot take place without engaged, enthusiastic team members.

In the supermarket industry, we have learned that we can improve sales by developing our own brands to replace generic brands. But if you simply create a brand and alter the packaging without providing an engaged team member to promote the product, the brand's full potential will never be realized.

29

For example, Harley-Davidson enjoys a strong emotional connection with its customers. What other company has customers who tattoo the company's brand name on their body—permanently? United sells a lot of green beans, but we have yet to see the Del Monte brand tattooed on a guest's chest. Harley-Davidson sells more than motorcycles. The company sells a lifestyle of adventure and excitement—universal ideals that appeal to hardcore bikers and accountants alike. Conventional supermarkets are just selling beans.

Similarly, Starbucks represents much more than coffee to its patrons. Its success is rooted in providing a refuge for guests—a place of comfort and familiarity that Starbucks founder Howard Schultz calls "the third place."

Companies spend millions to create a bond with customers, but pay little attention to making the same commitment to their own workforce. The reality is, if the workforce cannot deliver the goods of the campaign, customers will see through it immediately. A slick advertising campaign is not enough without a strong foundation of truth built on the organization's people.

Culture-driven organizations do more than lead with values; they seek to bring those values alive for people and partners. *Understanding higher math means recognizing that a slick ad campaign will lead to failure every time if the guest's experience does not match the expectation built by the ad.*

Consider the concept of business fidelity. On occasion, United sends team members to shop at other retailers and to see what they are offering. Not long ago, one of these people was shopping at a large discount store and found a product that United did not carry, so the team member took the product off the shelf and headed to the checkout, thinking about showing the product to United in an effort to place it in our stores.

The team member got in line with seven other shoppers who were waiting to be checked out. A large sign above the register made this promise: "Whenever there are three or more in line, we will open another register." The customers standing in the steadily growing line decided to ask management about honoring the pledge.

Within a few minutes, a manager appeared, and he was politely reminded about the sign. He looked at the sign and said, "Oh, yes, I apologize—I'll take care of it right away." About five minutes later, he reappeared with a ladder and—amazingly—took the sign down.

On the one hand, the manager's action was not what those in line were hoping for, but on the other hand, who could blame him? He knew that he did not have the labor force to make good on the promise, so he did the next best thing: he got rid of the sign. At least in that way he could reconcile the truth in his own mind—he was not going to open more registers.

31

People-centered organizations faithfully represent their mission 100 percent of the time. It is the simple idea of doing the right thing, which is the Golden Rule restated. For example, at United, we frame the Golden Rule in these terms: Do unto others as you would have your children done unto. That fulfills the human spirit and allows for connecting with people on a deeper level.

Moreover, when people connect emotionally, a high level of trust is developed. The responsibility for setting the tone in this area starts with the leader. Despite the simplicity of this thought, the American business culture typically scoffs at such idealistic thinking. It is far more fashionable to cast aside such universal truths as sentimental or hokey.

Consider this example from a 1995 United Supermarkets ad. We produced a 60-second television commercial saluting the American farmer. The spot chronicled a day in the life of one Texas farming family—father, mother, and two children. It did not mention any specific item that was on sale or give any information about deeply discounted prices—there was just a simple comment at the end of the commercial that said, "United Supermarkets salutes the American farmer."

The television commercial first aired on a Friday night during the local newscasts on all major networks. Almost immediately, industry peers and representatives from advertising agencies objected to it, citing the fact that there was no call to action.

United stood its ground. We believed that in our agriculture-dominated market, local farming families would connect with the message. They did. By Monday morning, we were inundated with calls of support. Hundreds of letters soon followed. We run the commercial every year because people call asking to see it.

33

Dr. Leonard Berry, whom I hold in high regard professionally, is a marketing expert on the topic of customer service. The book *Discovering the Soul of Service* is among his most highly regarded works because it contains a comprehensive model that reveals the soul beneath great service companies. Note the reference to "soul" in the book's title—it is a word chosen wisely after years of research.

Dr. Berry's findings reveal a common denominator among world-class, people-centered organizations that is inspiring and humbling. The best of the best understand the creation of a service-oriented environment is not necessarily delivered by a perceptive business initiative, but is delivered by an ongoing commitment to humane values.

Exactly what is the net gain of humane values? Where do they appear on the profit-and-loss statement? In truth, you will not find such values quantified on a financial report. They reside in the people you employ and the customers they serve. *If Walt Disney were still alive, he might refer to this as the "pixie dust" of business—that marvelous moment when you realize you have created a sustainable culture, one that is built to serve others, is rooted in humane values, and is marked by a high level of trust.* Then and only then can the human spirit be unleashed and the organization be catapulted to new heights.

34

When that moment occurs, the human engine of innovation and inspiration begins creating an unlimited supply of energy, constantly refueling itself and delivering remarkable sustainability. People begin identifying with the higher purpose and come to know the joy of fulfilling work. People-centered organizations connect the work they are doing with the mission they are committed to accomplishing.

A sustainable culture-driven, people-centered enterprise exists when team members take ownership of what they are doing and realize it is important and essential to the higher purpose. In the case of Medtronic, a company that reflects these values, employees have come to understand the life they save might just be that of a coworker.

FROM THE EXPRESS LANE

- ❋ Higher math means paying attention to people with the same fervor with which you pay attention to profits.

- ❋ Today's profit-driven business model is fatally flawed.

- ❋ Business leaders must be emotionally engaged with people throughout their organization.

- ❋ Merchants thrive on challenge; storekeepers suffocate in the status quo.

- ❋ Business fidelity means connected team members deliver the goods to satisfied customers.

- ❋ Engaging the souls of team members allows for the genuine engagement of guests.

THE EMERGING CAREER MODEL

The best part of the United Supermarkets CEO's day is going into the stores and interacting with team members and guests. These meetings always provide an opportunity to learn and serve as a reminder of how much I do not know about everyday store operations. As a rule, chief executives receive filtered information in small bits. I know from experience that if I do not consistently make it into the stores, the chance of candid feedback finding its way to the corner office is remote.

I recall one particular routine trip to a store. I walked the aisles, spent time with guests, thanked team members, and learned what was working and what was not. As my visit ended, a young man in a neatly pressed United Supermarkets uniform approached me. "Mr. Sanders," he said, "this is my first day on the job, and I want to introduce myself."

We spent only a short amount of time getting acquainted before he asked this interesting question: "How long do you think it will be before I'm promoted to store director?"

His query caught me off guard, primarily because he had been a team member for all of four hours.

I responded, "That's an interesting question. Why do you ask?"

His answer was an epiphany. "I want to be in charge so that I can make a difference," he said.

As I thought about his comment, I wondered what we had done in our culture to lead people, young and old, to believe that they must climb to the top of an organization before they can make a difference. I took a small piece of paper and drew two pictures. One represented the old career model; the second represented a new career model.

By the time we finished, this young man knew what I believe to be the truth regarding career progression and making a difference. People can make a difference in an organization, regardless of position or salary, as long as they grasp the organization's vision and mission.

THE PEOPLE-CENTERED CULTURE relies on leaders who genuinely connect with team members. At United, we believe connecting is the key to establishing a sustainable culture because it requires going beyond surface issues. Just as the body is covered with skin, organizations are covered with the most recent financial performance. In other words, the skin represents the numbers. Sustainable, culture-driven organizations go beyond the skin to the heart and soul of their people.

Connected team members understand the organization's vision and mission. Because of that, they recognize the unique importance of their own specific role. In the supermarket business, we have thousands of opportunities each day to make a difference for guests. For example, each day we make birthday cakes for guests and their loved ones. When cake decorators fill an order, they realize it is more than just another cake request—it is an opportunity to breathe life into a significant moment in someone's life. Virtually any grocery store will make a cake; I like to think no one does it with United's attention to detail. Its decorators know that their cake, along with the celebration of family and friends, will be memorialized in a photo album for a lifetime.

In the same way, our florists understand that each arrangement is special. During the course of a day, they will play a central role in celebrating a couple's anniversary, wishing best of luck at a grand opening for a local business, brightening the day of a cancer patient, and paying tribute with a funeral spray to a beloved friend after his or her passing. Which of these orders would we consider "routine"? At United, if we are connected to the emotions associated with each, the only answer is, "none."

Professional satisfaction is derived from serving others, not from posturing for the next promotion. Deep meaning and job fulfillment can be found in abundance if an organization's culture is on target.

The old career model is recognized for what it is: a misguided notion of what has come to be called "the American Dream" but has been exported around the world. Prevailing organizational wisdom today suggests one must start at the bottom and slowly climb the corporate ladder before making a real difference. Unfortunately, that model results in disengaged team members and costly turnover.

The old career model implies the best job in the company is that of the CEO because it represents the pinnacle of workplace achievement. Once someone is promoted to the top position, popular culture would suggest, "You've made it! You've won the prize!" Given that CEO turnover rates reach record levels nearly every year, I jokingly wonder whether aspiring to be a CEO is an intelligent thing to do.

Global CEO turnover reached record levels in 2005, quadruple the rate of turnover a decade earlier. It seems CEOs who live exclusively by the numbers die by the numbers.

The Old Career Progression Path

FINISH

$ $
$

START

$

Symbols of Success:
Money, Power, Materialism

The New Career Progression Path

Symbols of Success:
Humility, Selflessness, Fulfillment

A new career model is emerging. The new model suggests a different path to success. Unlike in the old model, team members begin making a difference their first day on the job; there is no such thing as a bottom rung on the ladder because no ladder exists. What does exist? Opportunities to serve. *Relationships represent the new currency, and cash compensation is no longer the primary indicator of success.*

The old career progression model's outright dependence on tangibles (money, power, and materialism) is replaced with a proper balance between the need for material gain and for intangibles (humility, selflessness, and fulfillment). The result is what people need most today: the ability to make a living while making a meaningful difference.

"The American Dream," which is commonly defined today as the pursuit of financial wealth and is characterized by excessive materialism, must give way to a higher calling. Organizations with a people-centered culture encourage individuals to live their lives aligned with godly values, which, in turn, make impossible dreams possible.

Of the two models illustrated in this chapter, which affords the better opportunity to make impossible dreams possible? Great things, even impossible things, occur when humans are connected to a higher purpose, one that is best represented in the new, emerging career model. Some of America's and the world's greatest accomplishments never would have transpired if people had not been connected to a higher purpose.

Engaged business leaders who are part of a culture-driven, people-centered enterprise understand the importance of talent and the bearing it has on the bottom line. As a result, addressing turnover is a high priority. For example, turnover is a constant battle in the supermarket business.

Regardless of their reasons for departing, we try to interview each team member prior to that individual's leaving our company. More than a decade ago, while serving as leader of our human resources team, I found almost all of the conversations were tied to the company's intangible benefits. In other words, hourly pay, auto allowances, and bonus compensation were rarely what people wanted to talk about—despite their importance.

Instead, from those who were moving toward something, such as a new career after graduation, we regularly heard about our family-oriented culture, the lifelong friendships forged at work, and the sense of accomplishment that came from taking care of our guests in stores. For those who were running from something, such as disappointment in the leader or some type of workplace personality conflict, we regularly heard about a failure to connect with the vision and the mission.

A great deal has happened around the world and especially in America since the early 1990s, but the leader of our human resources (now called talent management) team reminds our leaders regularly intangibles cannot be underestimated because of the impact they have on predictable behavior.

44

I first met Dr. John Gourville in 2003 while I was attending an executive education program in marketing at Harvard Business School. Harvard's reputation for assembling great thinkers is well known, but until you enroll in a program, you might not fully appreciate the school's remarkable commitment to knowledge.

During our marketing discussion, Dr. Gourville spent time describing his ideas regarding the psychology of gains and losses, developed from source material from Amos Tversky, the late Stanford psychology professor, and Daniel Kahneman, a Princeton psychology professor and Nobel laureate.

45

The psychology of gains and losses describes the challenges involved in identifying predictable behavior. Drs. Tversky and Kahneman's study findings suggest that human beings are constantly evaluating the outcomes of gains and losses. Additionally, their findings show these three interesting facts:

1. There is a decreasing marginal utility of gains and losses.
2. There is a greater fear of loss than desire for gain.
3. There is a reference point, and it is often the "status quo."

Dr. Gourville provided the illustration below, graphically depicting a person's psychological processing of a $5,000 raise. The graph to the left shows the raise given in January 2006, whereas the graph at the right illustrates the person's psychological position a year later. Not surprisingly, the $5,000 increase is now considered the "status quo." In other words, as 2007 rolls round, the psychological value of last year's raise is no longer seen as a gain.

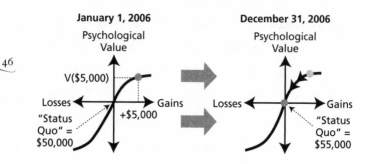

Companies that deal only with the skin, the outer issues, attempt to solve morale problems with money (tangible cash compensation), rather than investing time and energy into understanding the culture (intangible lifestyle factors). It is customary these days to base cash compensation on performance; however, consider alternatives where the psychological value is not lost. Trips and special events are a great way to recognize achievement and acknowledge team members throughout an organization.

In my varied professional career, I have seen a wide variety of nontraditional incentives used to establish a personal connection with team members. Here are just a few meaningful examples, some of which we have used at United:

1. Distribute tickets to concerts or local entertainment events, and allow team members to invite family and friends.
2. Lease a cabin in the mountains or on a beach, and allow team members to take their families and friends for a week at a time.
3. Lease a private suite for a college or professional sporting event and allow team members to bring their families.
4. Provide a team member with a gift card and a personal word of thanks.
5. Send a team member and his or her spouse on a romantic getaway.
6. Hire a professional photographer to take a formal family portrait. Have it framed to match the team member's home décor.

7. Assemble a gift basket with items special to a team member, and then hand carry the package to the team member's office or home.

8. Purchase a book about a topic that you know to be of interest to a team member. Write a short, personal note on the inside cover, and send the book through the mail to the team member's home.

9. Provide free movie tickets with coupons for concession items.

10. Select a clothier to provide a team member with a custom-tailored outfit.

In each of these examples, the thought and the memory are far more important than the actual cash compensation. Our leadership team voted in 2005 to meet with every person in the company, say "thank you," and hand that person a crisp $100 bill. We covered the tax so the team member did not have to worry about it. We had team members throughout the company comment afterward that it was the most meaningful day of their careers, not because of the cash, but because of the personal word of thanks that accompanied the payout.

I like to remind team members we have thousands of CEOs in the company, whether you are working in the corner office or carrying groceries to a guest's vehicle. *Everyone is empowered in a people-centered culture.* We want team members to feel empowered to own their part in what is a complex company composed of thousands of parts. We are interdependent—no part is unimportant. No effective CEO would deny this.

From time to time, I hear someone suggest that one job is more important than another, but this simply is not the case. The most gifted store director will not stay engaged long if the team at the distribution center fails to get product to the store. The team at the distribution center cannot accomplish what it must do if truck drivers are not ready to take the load.

Moreover, the truck drivers most likely will not continue driving if the payroll clerk fails to process their checks. One might argue the most important job in the company is not that of CEO, but that of payroll clerk.

In truth, all team members need to do their part, making the difference that only they can make. *This is the beauty of a people-centered culture: each team member is celebrated, not because of his or her position, but because of the unique contribution from that team member.*

Consider this example: Each year I attend a number of receptions for team members in our company who have spent 30 or more years in a position. Not long ago, I attended a reception recognizing a checker's thirty-fifth anniversary with the company. She had been at the same store, working in the same checkout lane, for the past 35 years.

The reception was attended by hundreds of people who had grown up with this checker. In some cases, she had served three generations of the same family. In addition to our team members, a large number of guests came to express their gratitude.

I was astonished that someone could serve in the same role for that length of time and maintain a steady sense of joy, fulfillment, and satisfaction. I asked her about her motivation and dedication to service, what kept her will to serve burning. Her response was telling in that she never felt like she was going to work. "I know all of these people, and I care about all of these people," she said. "I have a relationship with these families, and they have a relationship with me. This isn't work. This is my joy."

I was inspired to see firsthand that a team member considered her work a faithful response to God. For this particular individual, her desire to please God helped her find significance.

In popular culture, this team member who had spent her life checking out groceries would be considered just another moving part in a profit machine, but in a people-centered organization, she is an inspiration—a hero!

FROM THE EXPRESS LANE

- ✳ Connecting reduces turnover and inspires team members to galvanize the organization.
- ✳ Organizations focused on people encourage individuals to live their lives aligned with godly values, which, in turn, makes impossible dreams possible.
- ✳ Intangibles are exceedingly important because they drive predictable behavior, not rational behavior.
- ✳ Everyone is empowered in a culture-driven, people-centered organization.

MAKING
WINNERS FAIL

Those who are around us shape us. The people in our lives are a major influence on who we are, what we believe, and what we do. Traveling to new places and experiencing different cultures enhances this process. We cannot help but be changed—sometimes for good, and other times for bad. This is one of life's common denominators.

Don Peterson permanently changed my life. A retired lieutenant general, he is the executive director of the Air Force Association and Aerospace Education Foundation. General Peterson's military career was exceptional. Besides amassing more than 4,000 flying hours, including almost 600 combat hours in high-performance aircraft, he commanded a tactical fighter squadron, a tactical fighter wing, and a flying training wing. He also commanded the Cheyenne Mountain Operations Center of the North American Aerospace Defense Command and U.S. Space Command. The man is a great leader.

I first met General Peterson in 1991 at Randolph Air Force Base in San Antonio, Texas. He was the commander of the Twelfth Flying Training Wing at that time. I was a captain assigned to his staff as one of his executive officers. In the military, an executive officer is competent at everything, from making coffee to writing speeches. It is not a glamorous position, but the trade-off is that executive officers have remarkable access to senior leaders much earlier in their careers than their peers, which makes the role worthwhile.

One late afternoon in the spring of 1992, I happened to be standing with General Peterson looking out a window in his office. His office provided a panoramic view of most of the activity on the base because it was atop the building affectionately referred to as "The Taj," short for Taj Mahal. The building stood between parallel runways, one used primarily for T-38 jets and one used primarily for T-37 jets. General Peterson made an

*insightful observation as we stood there shoulder to
shoulder watching the jets take off on their
respective training missions.*

*"The average age of the instructor pilot in each
one of those jets taking off is about 25," he said.
"They're flying multimillion-dollar airplanes,
carrying with them student instructor pilots still
learning the trade, and with every mission my career
is on the line." I looked at the general and asked,
"How is it that your career is on the line when they
are responsible for what happens?" He responded,
"As the leader, you can delegate authority, but you
can never delegate responsibility."*

IT WAS A POIGNANT MOMENT for me—a leadership
lesson seared into my consciousness forever. As the
leader, General Peterson had delegated authority to his
instructor pilots to fly the Air Force's jets and train
their students, but the ultimate responsibility was his
and his alone.

Not unlike the world of sports, where a losing
team results in a new coach before it results in new
players, poor execution in an organization results in
a new CEO before it results in new team members.

For this reason, successful leaders truly belong to their followers.

Quite often, leaders get this concept reversed—they embrace a misguided notion that their followers are their property. Such thinking is destructive because it is impossible to build a culture-driven, people-centered organization without understanding that serving others helps them realize their potential.

In a context of personal faith, serving others is called servanthood. For this reason, many leaders avoid thinking of servanthood in a secular way. Certainly, the modern view advocates separating anything that might be considered faith-based from things that are secular-based. In many cases, the courts, politicians, and educational scholars endorse this view.

Therefore, many leaders today resist using the concept of servanthood in the day-to-day management of organizations because they fear that the concept blurs the lines between religion and secularism. Some critics even suggest servanthood is rooted in negativism because it creates too much focus on people's shortcomings.

For example, critics argue that churches, social service organizations, and medical practitioners cannot realize a sense of servanthood unless they fix the problems facing the people they serve. They suggest that servanthood toward humanity cannot happen without identifying a person's weaknesses—his or her specific failures, poor decisions, or destructive habits.

We at United Supermarkets believe that servanthood is about helping others realize their potential by focusing not on their weaknesses but on their strengths. Those who choose to lead, regardless of their position in an organization, have a responsibility to help people prepare to make the most of the opportunities afforded them.

The most effective way to succeed at servanthood is to mentor people, improving their capacity to contribute in a meaningful manner. *When leaders are actively mentoring and modeling our culture, they are assuring its sustainability and building communities connected by an emotional bond that will prevail for generations.*

Culture-driven, people-centered leaders understand the importance of finding an inspirational connection from their past. Although I have lived in many places, I am a devout Texan. My childhood memories include many trips to see the Alamo in San Antonio, where Texan and Tejano volunteers fought against Mexican troops during the Texas Revolution.

57

In 1836, nearly 200 defenders, including William Travis, James Bowie, and David Crockett, held out for 13 days against Santa Anna's army. For generations of Texans, the battle has symbolized heroism, sacrifice, and servanthood. Eventually, Texans gained their liberty, and the Alamo became hallowed ground—the undisputed cradle of Texas independence.

Odd as it might seem, asking my two children what they remember most about waking up and going to school would prompt the response that most mornings I whispered in their ears, "I love you, and Jesus loves you, too" and "Remember the Alamo!" Why would I choose such statements?

First, as the leader of my family, I wanted them both to know, regardless of what might happen that day, that I loved them and that their Creator loved them. Second, I wanted them to feel an emotional connection in knowing that, for Texans, the Alamo serves as a symbol of the extraordinary opportunities that they have to do something meaningful with their lives. It was one way of connecting my children to the living memory of those brave defenders—a celebration of their strength and their selflessness.

Servanthood is merely a starting point. A willingness to mentor and help others realize their potential ultimately causes friendship to blossom. It is one thing to be a servant, but it is something entirely different to be a friend. Followers of Christ, for example, might consider the distinction made by Jesus himself near the end of his life on earth.

During the Last Supper, just prior to his crucifixion, Jesus said, "I no longer call you servants, because servants do not know the business of the one they serve. But I have called you friends because I have made known to you everything I learned from God." It is an interesting statement, considering Jesus' example. In essence, servanthood comes first, developing a fertile field from which relationships, trust, compassion, understanding, and friendship grow.

Like timeless, universal truths, servanthood and friendship are always welcomed. This is not a question of religion, yet many people want to make it such. I believe servanthood and the friendship that stems from it are often trivialized when efforts are made to associate such thinking with one religion or another. Frankly, I believe these truths transcend arguments regarding doctrine or denominationalism. They bring us to a greater understanding of God's love for people. My role is not to condemn or condone, but to seek commonality first. What seems important to me is not what drives us apart but what binds us together.

Whether this is seen from a spiritual or a secular vantage point, we all need the encouragement of fellowship. It would be a pity to deny the benefits of servanthood and friendship because of differences of opinion regarding the precise "religious" origin of such behavior. I believe that someday we will learn the answer to the question from God himself. Until then, perhaps we can all spend less time worrying over what to condemn and what to condone and simply serve one another with spirit-lifting love and genuine friendship.

The leaders of culture-driven, people-centered organizations embrace such thinking, which is why leaders move so quickly to surround themselves with friends—people they can trust. An outsider looking in might argue that such moves are a reflection of the cronyism often found in politics or established institutions. Regrettably, sometimes that is the case. More often, it is simply the leader assembling a trusted team that can influence the organization quickly. Why is this so important?

General Peterson's belief that leaders cannot delegate responsibility requires leaders to create teams capable of being empowered with the organization's mission. Otherwise, how can any leader possibly be comfortable shouldering responsibility for everything that conceivably might happen today, tomorrow, or the next day?

United Supermarkets team members serve more than one million guests each week. As the company's CEO, it is my responsibility to ensure each guest leaves satisfied. Imagine the stress of dealing with that kind of responsibility without relationships, trust, compassion, or understanding in the workplace. On the other hand, imagine the power of more than 9,000 friends—people with whom I have served and whom I have mentored—serving more than one million guests each week.

From General Peterson's perspective, *the leader's ability to understand servanthood and friendship is the difference between a career that flounders and a career that flourishes.*

Subscribing to a leadership style that begins with servanthood and develops friendships means eradicating harsh and unfair treatment of people. In a culture-driven, people-centered organization, leaders have a clear understanding of the difference between a mistake and a crime. We all make mistakes, including leaders. A crime is an entirely different story. A crime is a malicious act in violation of the culture or the organization's values.

Team members who commit crimes cannot be allowed to stay. Team members who make mistakes remain team members because forgiveness has a legitimate place in organizations, just as in families.

The idea that leaders get more out of people by screaming obscenities at them is ludicrous and unsustainable. Even so, it is not uncommon. For example, some sports coaches rationalize their unprofessional behavior by claiming an enviable winning record, and the culture seems amused by the ideology until they start losing games; then it becomes less amusing.

Coaches who accept the truth—that they belong to their players—most likely will treat their players like friends and not like property. Friendship means much more than simply what one person can do for another. It is an emotional investment in each other's lives, creating a special bond, a common journey.

Larry Hays is the head baseball coach at Texas Tech University and the former head coach at Lubbock Christian University. In 2005, he became just the fourth coach in NCAA history to record 1,400 wins. A nine-time Coach of the Year, Hays was elected to the NAIA Hall of Fame. Major League baseball teams have drafted more than 100 of his players.

I was a 17-year-old pitching prospect when I first met Coach Hays in 1977 on the Lubbock Christian campus, where we discussed the possibility of a baseball scholarship. At the time, Lubbock Christian did not have a baseball field of its own. The team practiced and played at various diamonds around the city. It seemed odd to me that Lubbock Christian's baseball team—a team ranked number four in the nation among NAIA schools—had no facility.

Coach Hays proved to be different from the start. Unlike coaches at other universities, who provided tours of their baseball facilities and spoke to me in detail about their baseball programs, Hays had no facility to tour and spent little time talking about baseball. Instead, we talked about my hopes and desires in life. I am certain we talked baseball at some point; however, most of what I recall had to do with Coach Hays's servanthood—his genuine desire to figure out if he could help me realize my potential as a person. I was impressed.

I returned to Houston and excitedly reported that I had committed to attend Lubbock Christian.

"What's their stadium like?" my dad asked.

"They don't have a stadium," I replied.

"Where do they practice?" Dad asked.

"I'm not sure," I said.

"Did you get a full scholarship?" he asked.

"I'm not sure what kind of scholarship I'm getting," I remarked.

My dad, the engineer, tried to summarize, "Hmmm, no stadium, no practice facility, no scholarship details—so why do you want to go there?"

With great confidence, I said, "Coach Larry Hays—he cares about me as a person, not just as a baseball player."

Coach Hays's servanthood-first approach led to a lasting friendship. During my four years at Lubbock Christian, we won nearly 200 games. We made it to the NAIA World Series in 1980. During that period, I never saw Coach Hays lose his temper, hurl an obscenity, or conduct himself unprofessionally.

He treated every player with respect and, by doing so, enjoyed good relationships and a high level of trust with his players. Communication was a two-way street, and we truly worked together to deliver superior performance. Losses were learning opportunities, not life-destroying events. Coach Hays had a higher purpose than just coaching baseball.

Not surprisingly, Lubbock Christian regretted losing Coach Hays to Texas Tech, but not for the reason you might think. Lubbock Christian was worried not because of the potential impact on the school's remarkable baseball program, but because of the potential impact on the school's enviable history of producing successful graduates in a program that embodied the ideals of the university.

Since entering the business world, I often have reflected on Coach Hays's impact on my life. His character-driven example helps me understand that treating people harshly and unfairly is symptomatic of a leader's anxiety over knowing that he or she cannot delegate responsibility to someone else. Without investing the time necessary to establish relationships, an organization's leaders will never realize that difficult-to-reach level of trust and peace.

65

I am certain Larry Hays sometimes wishes he could jump out on the field and fix a player's problem. Fortunately, *once the relationships are established, the friendships are formed, and the teaching is under way, a leader learns the important lesson of letting go.*

Many of America's greatest leaders understand the interdependent nature of these elements. The order in which people are exposed to the servanthood and mentoring process is important. *Great leaders understand servanthood comes first, before mentoring and friendship. In sustainable organizations, connecting what people do on a daily basis with the higher purpose is paramount.*

The degree to which that connection resonates with the workforce is directly proportional to the degree to which the workforce feels a part of the community. The word *community* implies a sense of sharing in common—a sense of family. Servanthood leadership establishes precisely the kind of community that embraces a culture-driven, people-centered organization.

Sometimes leaders rush to judgment where their people are concerned. They promote talented team members too quickly and wonder why things do not work out. This is an easy mistake to make because at the heart of the matter is a desire to help someone make the most of an opportunity.

We have made these kinds of mistakes at United. For example, we employ exceptionally talented meat cutters to work in our meat markets. They are masters at cutting the perfect rib-eye steak or trimming the ideal brisket.

That can set the stage innocently for this scenario: we need a market manager for a new store we are opening. The market supervisors get together and discuss the matter. Understandably, they start with a short list of candidates known for their beef-cutting skills.

Following a series of interviews, the successful candidate is assigned to the new store. Sometime after the grand opening, feedback from the store suggests we may have a problem with our new market manager. The team investigates and determines the new market manager schedules poorly and struggles with people issues. Sadly, the team thinks it best to make a change; the new market manager is demoted. He leaves demoralized, feeling as though his career is over.

So, by now you may be asking the question, "Did anyone assess whether the market manager had the skills necessary to serve in a management role or teach him those skills?" After all, managing people requires a set of skills vastly different from those needed to cut beef. The answers are self-critiquing.

People are promoted not for what they have done but for what they can do. When promoting someone to a new position, do so with the confidence that the person has the skills to succeed in that position. It is not enough to say someone was good in the past; the person has to be good in the future.

If someone is a good meat cutter, but does not have the soft skills needed to be a manager, recognize and applaud him for being a great meat cutter. But do not promote him to a management position until you have enabled him to develop his leadership skills.

You need to understand leaders can make winners fail. It happens all the time, and it is unfair. Mentoring team members—grooming them to be promoted—is crucial to any organization. The military is one group particularly adept at mapping out careers. It is common for general officers leading huge enterprises to manage the careers of their junior officers. I recall working with one general officer who carried a briefcase for personnel matters. It contained a magnetic board inside with the names of junior officers printed on small tabs.

Remarkably, the board contained the general's plan for the organization's leadership positions 10, 15, and 20 years in the future. In painstaking detail, each stop a junior officer would need to make to obtain the expertise required for the plan was laboriously laid out on the board.

Some junior officers were young captains in the infancy of their careers. They had distinguished themselves enough to catch the general's eye. Of course, changes were certain when officers separated from the service early or opted for different careers. Despite that, it is important to recognize the planning process typically ensured talented officers promoted to higher levels of responsibility had a greater likelihood of achieving success.

One reason I am passionate about equipping people for success is I had superb mentors who helped me take advantage of my opportunities. My father was not so fortunate. Throughout his entire life, he took on the personal responsibility for obtaining new skills. A Depression-era child, he grew up in a rural community. Disenchanted by farm life, he graduated early from high school and, at age 16, enrolled at Texas Tech in 1946. Four years later, he graduated and entered the oil business with Pan American, later Amoco and now British Petroleum.

For the next 35 years, he worked as a staff engineer in domestic production and international exploration. Twenty years after he joined the company, he noticed a trend: the company promoted employees who were gifted speakers noticeably faster than other employees. It occurred to him that engineers or geologists capable of distilling complex information in a manner easily understood had a distinct advantage when it came to promotions.

69

To his credit, and with little assistance from his supervisor or the company, he enrolled in a Dale Carnegie course on public speaking. While he was a whiz at mathematics, he knew he lacked confidence when it was time to make presentations to the company's top management. I vividly recall seeing my dad practice in front of the mirror, struggling with his hand gestures and the tips learned from the course.

His initiative left a lasting impression on me. When I prepared to leave for college, he said, "Make certain you take as many speech and debate classes as you can." When I arrived for my first year at Lubbock Christian, I immediately sought out E. Don Williams, a professor of communications. "Dr. Williams," I said, "I absolutely must learn to speak in public."

Dr. Williams mentored me the next four years. A gifted speaker himself, Dr. Williams ensured that I participated in speech competitions at universities and colleges across the country. In addition to videotaping my talks, he would put me through my paces with impromptu subject matter on which I had just a moment to collect my thoughts and present a speech.

In retrospect, this was a wonderful blessing and a clear example of mentoring. Following graduation, I was hired at the local ABC affiliate to anchor the weekend news. From there, I entered the military, where I was afforded the opportunity to deliver the wing mission briefing to foreign dignitaries and senior political leaders.

After I left active duty and entered business, my skill at public speaking was one tool I had at my disposal for completing company acquisitions. In my role today, I view communicating effectively with our team among my most important responsibilities. Without the mentoring I received from Dr. Williams, I am not certain such opportunities would have come my way. For this reason, my friendship with Dr. Williams is among many treasured gifts from my alma mater.

71

As leaders, we must resist the temptation to promote winners before they are ready. *The success of team members rests on our willingness to take the time to forge relationships by first exhibiting servanthood—a genuine desire to help others make the most of their potential.* Such commitment is not easy, and we cannot delegate this responsibility to others. It requires an investment of our most precious asset: time.

The rewards, however, are significant and lasting. After servanthood come mentoring, friendship, and the understanding that comes from knowing you played a key role in helping a winner win.

FROM THE EXPRESS LANE

- Leaders can delegate authority, but they can never delegate responsibility.
- We are influenced by those around us; choose carefully by whom you wish to be influenced.
- Great leaders understand the important role servant leadership plays in helping others realize their potential.
- Servant leadership requires time and patience, resulting in building relationships and friendships based on trust.
- Leaders must discern when team members are ready for promotion.
- It is the leader's job to ensure winners on the team win.

TELLING PLAYERS FROM FANS

Britain Brewer is a store director for United. I gained an appreciation for his talents in the summer of 1997, when he was serving as an assistant store director. During one of my routine store visits, I found myself face to face with trouble. An elderly farmer wearing tattered overalls and sporting a well-worn John Deere ball cap walked into the store and came straight to me.

"I've come to town from my farm about an hour away, and I need my juice," he said. Of course, I had no idea what he was talking about, but I could tell he had something specific in mind. "What kind of juice do you like?" I asked. "It comes in a bottle," he replied.

Knowing how many juices we sell in bottles, I decided the easiest thing to do was walk with the man to the juice department so we could find it through the process of elimination. However, before I could share my plan, the farmer said, "I had it special ordered several weeks ago for my wife."

"Oh, I see," I said. "Do you know who you spoke with regarding the special order?"

The farmer thought for a moment and then said, "No, I don't have any idea." I offered the farmer a seat and a cup of coffee and then proceeded to the office in hopes of identifying the team member who had taken his special order. The first person I ran into was the point-of-sale clerk. "Do you know who might have taken a special order for juice for a farmer living outside of town?" I asked. She thought for a moment and replied, "Yes, I remember. Britain Brewer took that gentleman's order."

As you might expect, her answer provided the relief I was looking for. "Where's Britain?" I asked. "Britain is on vacation and can't be reached," she said. My heart sank. My relief was short-lived. I searched the back room for anything that looked as if it might be a special order for juice, but had no luck. By now, I was emotionally preparing myself to walk onto the sales floor and explain to the farmer that his one-hour commute to the store was going to result in no special-ordered juice.

As I gathered my thoughts, one of our young sackers stopped me and asked, "Are you looking for some juice?"

"Yes, I am! Do you know where it is?" I exclaimed.

"Yes," the young man said, "Britain was leaving for vacation this morning, but he came by the store before he left and set the juice aside with a note taped to it."

The sacker took me to the front of the store and a small office used for storage; immediately, I spotted the juice with the label.

On the note was written: "This juice is a special order for Mrs. Atwood. I expect her husband will pick it up while I am on vacation. Britain Brewer, Assistant Manager." The burden was lifted, thanks to Britain's conscientiousness—even in the face of a family eager to go on vacation. I proudly presented the juice to Mr. Atwood and thanked him for shopping United. When I returned to the office, I made a note to myself regarding what had happened. "Britain Brewer," I wrote, "is a player, not a fan."

ORGANIZATIONS ARE LIKE TEAMS, and teams attract fans. In fact, teams are composed of players and fans. Players represent the team every day of the week because, whether or not they are playing, they are still a part of the team. Players are apprised of the team's strategies and tactics, know the "playbook," and take ownership of their role in the overall success of each play. Players wear the same uniform as other team members, not one of their choosing. They rely on one another for support, and they recognize and embrace their teammates' strengths. They win together and lose together. They exude camaraderie, loyalty, and unity.

On the other hand, fans are fickle. If the team is winning, they are happy. If the team is losing, they are unhappy—sometimes very unhappy. Fans like to offer advice, yet the overwhelming majority have never played the game. They wear whatever makes them feel good that day; they have even been known to paint their faces or wear costumes in hopes of catching a television producer's attention and getting two or three seconds on camera. Fans are like outdoor pennants fastened to stadium poles—they flutter in the same direction as the prevailing breeze.

In the early 1970s, McCoy McLemore, a professional basketball player, moved into a house directly across the street from my house in Houston. At the time, McLemore was playing for the NBA's Milwaukee Bucks. However, a trade to bring him to the Houston Rockets was already in the works. Since I was a high school basketball player at the time, the idea of a professional basketball player as my neighbor was a dream come true.

McLemore proved to be exceptionally nice to me. In addition to introducing me to some of the NBA's greatest players, he routinely invited me to pro clinics, autograph sessions, and Rockets games. McLemore drove a Lincoln Continental that seemed 20 yards long to me. His personalized license plate read: NBA.

Houston was slow to warm to the Rockets. Crowds were generally small and surprisingly vocal. In those days, the Rockets played at Hofheinz Pavilion, a small arena built primarily for the University of Houston Cougars. I recall Rudy Tomjanovich, an emerging star at that time, saying once that several players were sitting on the bench talking about where they wanted to go eat after the game. "It was so quiet," Tomjanovich said, "a guy way up in the stands yells out, 'No, no, don't go there. That's not a good place to eat.'"

To be sure, seats were not hard to come by. One night, McLemore invited me to a game against a division rival. During the game, it seemed as if one of

McLemore's teammates, a rookie guard and future star missed every shot he took. Despite repeated attempts to score, he could not buy a basket—clearly a case of a rare off night for a player whose stock was rising otherwise. Despite the close game, the fans in attendance became increasingly irritated.

Since I had special credentials from McLemore, my seat next to the Rockets bench placed me just a few feet from the target of their hostility, and I watched as the player remained focused on the game. Some mean-spirited Houston fans hurled insults at the talented guard, and several appeared ready to throw cups of beer on him at every timeout. I had never seen such treatment of a player by fans in my life. As it turned out, the target of their hostility found himself at the free throw line with a chance to win the game that night. The Rockets trailed by one point.

He had two free throws. If he made both, the Rockets would win. The player took dead aim, even as some of the more vocal hometown fans continued to shout threats. "Swoosh!" Nothing but net. With the score tied, the fans' mood suddenly changed. They began chanting his name.

The young player paused as he looked at the basket. He bounced the basketball twice on the floor, focused for a brief moment, and sank the second free throw to secure the win. Several fans who had hurled insults downed the last of their beer and ran onto the floor, hoping to pick the hero up and carry him around on their shoulders. Security intervened. That moment convinced me that fans can be tough to please from one minute to the next, and players must be focused to avoid distractions.

That night, on the way back from the game, I asked McLemore if it bothered him to hear so many Houston fans acting poorly. I could tell by his expression that he was not fazed—successful pro athletes focus on winning, not on fans. That is part of what makes them professionals.

Organizations are similar; only the problem is worse. *In organizations, fans actually infiltrate the team, interfering with the players focused on getting the job done.* Often, they dress in the same uniform as the players, so security cannot readily differentiate between players and fans. In organizations, fans attend meetings, make sales calls, prepare reports, and even claim job titles, but they are nothing more than impostors—fans masquerading as players.

Looking at an organization's hiring process often reveals how impostors are able to enter organizations successfully. Far too many organizations subscribe to a "needs-based" approach to hiring. In other words, no serious recruiting, interviewing, or actual hiring of talent takes place until a specific need arises. This approach is especially popular in numbers-oriented cultures because the organization is measuring itself against a predetermined published labor budget for the quarter.

A needs-based operation creates complicated and drawn-out procedures requiring multiple approvals before any additional employees can be hired. The time between identifying the need for a new person and receiving approval to make the hire causes a steadily increasing strain on team members because they are shorthanded. Once approval is granted, the shorthanded team is so eager for help—of any kind— that a decision is made to hire a "warm body," with little time given to assessment of the individual, which is the same as allowing a fan on the team.

Hiring "warm bodies" allows impostors to penetrate organizations. Too often, "warm bodies" fail to appreciate the organization's vision, much less its values. *Ultimately, needs-based operational management handicaps a team's ability to win before it ever faces the competition.*

Culture-driven, people-centered organizations adopt a healthier approach. They are always looking for players, even if no need exists. This requires a commitment to scout for players, but the time is well spent. Players make immediate contributions without tearing the cultural fabric of the organization. On the other hand, impostors rarely contribute more than dissent and disdain.

Unfortunately, leaders are often the last to see impostors at work. Team members forced to work next to an imposter quickly recognize it. When leaders finally see the problem and remove the impostor, others in the organization respond with this remark: "What took you so long?"

Imagine allowing three fans to suit up for the Dallas Cowboys' next game. How long would it take for veteran Cowboys players to identify the impostors? My guess is the players, face to face with one another, would figure it out in the huddle. Coaches, watching from a distance, might want to see a few plays. Regrettably, the larger the team, the more difficult it becomes to differentiate players from fans—impostors from players.

Our best hires at United are products of multiple interviews, skill assessments, reference checks, and auditions for guest contact roles—the process is slow when compared to the "warm-body" hiring approach. Even so, the new hires' contributions to the team are worth the effort, and the reduction in turnover would make any accountant happy.

Even players sometimes become disenchanted, less interested in the team, and more concerned with their own achievement, which creates a second important issue. A visible example today comes from some professional athletes who engage in somewhat bizarre antics on and off the field. Such behavior is typically more about ego than about earnings. Professional agents schooled in the art of tough negotiating ensure that their clients are multimillionaires before they play a game. So, what happens to these talented stars? Why do players on teams—organizational teams, athletic or otherwise—get off track?

The answer can be found in an organizational model originally conceived by Dr. L. Ken Jones, president of Lubbock Christian University. Dr. Jones shared his findings with me in 1993 just as he was beginning to write his first book, *Leadership . . . After God's Own Heart*. His findings revealed great insights into the life cycle and leadership demands of organizations, families, and individuals.

Since our initial meeting, I have made slight modifications to the model to serve my own leadership needs. Even so, Dr. Jones discovered a model that is simple to grasp, universal in application, and strikingly accurate.

The model begins with a vision of who you are and a mission of what you want to achieve; this is true of all meaningful endeavors, personal and professional. In culture-driven, people-centered organizations, values serve as a litmus test for a leader's vision. If the vision violates or compromises those values, failure is likely. On the other hand, if the vision is aligned with the values, success is likely because goals and strategies bring about favorable results.

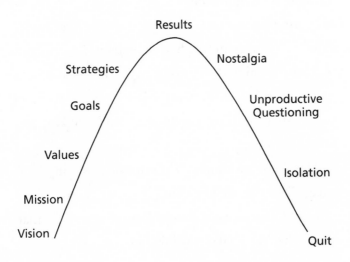

Life on the left side of the life-cycle curve is fulfilling because daily progress is made toward realizing the vision. For example, following my hospital stay in El Paso in the summer of 2006, I sat down with this model in front of me. My doctor recommended, because of my high blood pressure, I lose some weight. As a result, I created a new vision—one in which I was healthy. I also created a new mission—losing weight. Then I tested the vision and mission against my personal values. It made sense because my elevated blood pressure was threatening what I wanted to accomplish as a husband, father, and friend.

Next, I established the goal: lose 25 pounds. Finally, I plotted strategy; I committed to working out a minimum of three days each week while dramatically altering my diet. Not surprisingly, the weight came off. Fortunately, I had no extenuating circumstances to deal with regarding my weight-loss plan; I just needed to demonstrate self-restraint—no more steady diet of chips, candy bars, milk shakes, and fatty cheeseburgers.

This example simply illustrates how the model is used. With the weight gone, the importance of my original vision of being thinner is more important than ever. When my goal seemed daunting, I found encouragement and hope in reflecting on my vision of a thin me—a future with my wife, children, and friends.

Players with a clear vision will make great things happen. Players who have lost the vision creep over to the right side of the life-cycle curve.

It begins with nostalgic thinking. Saying, "Let's just go back to the way it used to be," is stage one of a four-stage process that results in total disengagement. The problem with nostalgic thinking is it presents an impossible solution. I remind team members and my family from time to time that going back is not an option.

For example, my daughter left in the late summer of 2006 for her first semester at Texas Christian University. At Thanksgiving, she returned home for a few days of relaxation and recreation. Shortly after arriving, she said, "Dad, things just seem different." I understood because I had felt the same way when I left home. It is true for everyone—once you have left home to pursue a college degree, a new job, or marriage, home will never be the same. It can still be pleasant, but it will never be what it was. Efforts to make it so are wasted motion.

Stage two of the journey prompts unproductive questioning, which tears down a healthy organization. Often, these are complaints disguised with question marks. For example, a team member might say, "Why do we have to keep this area so clean?" Is this a question or a statement? An answer is rarely warranted because the questions serve no constructive role in building up an organization.

Isolation continues the slide toward complete disengagement. We all have seen this stage with children on the playground. When things do not go their way, they walk away or isolate themselves from everyone else. If this stage had a slogan it might be, "I'm going to take my ball and go home." Worse yet, it might be, "I'm going to show up every day, but I'm not going to be present to work every day." Team members consumed with stage three are unhappy about everything. Stage three life is miserable.

If we are lucky, team members who reach stage three will eventually move on to stage four and quit, but, remarkably, people in stage three tend to hang on forever. It seems odd people so miserable would return each day and subject themselves to more misery, but all too often that is precisely what happens.

As leaders, we see the value of having everyone on the left side of the life-cycle curve—there is progress, fulfillment, and realization of a vision. So, how does a leader move people from the right-hand side of the curve back to the left-hand side of the curve?

First, in a culture-driven, people-centered organization, it is the leader's responsibility to remove impostors—to get the fans off the floor. Unfortunately, not everyone will move back to the curve's left-hand side. Leaders cannot allow a small number of fans to change the course of the game or distract the players from successfully attaining the team's goals.

Second, everyone creeps over to the right-hand side of the curve from time to time, but most of us choose not to stay there. When we find ourselves distracted, the answer to getting back on the positive side of the graph is to refocus and re-embrace the vision—this is the key, the answer. The vision is everything when it comes to moving team members from ineffectiveness to effectiveness. *Culture-driven, people-centered organizations never stop talking about their vision.*

Dr. Jones's discovery validates what should be apparent to anyone who has spent any time in the business world. *Selfish pride can destroy us all if we allow it.* In every stage of the life-cycle curve's road to total disengagement, selfishness and prideful thinking are present.

Sadly, in a numbers-oriented world, such issues often fail to capture the interest of senior leaders, analysts, or shareholders because these people have no commitment to differentiating between players and fans. Telling as they are, spreadsheets can reveal only so much. To prevent fans from masquerading as players, leaders need to hire intentionally, build relationships genuinely, and respect the trust among their players honorably. This philosophy creates a different kind of bottom line, the difference between winning and losing over the long term.

FROM THE EXPRESS LANE

❀ Players buy the mission; fans undermine it.

❀ People-centered organizations are always scouting for players; they never wait until they have a need.

❀ Players know how to keep ego and earnings in perspective.

❀ The leader is responsible for removing impostors before they damage the organization and its players.

❀ Pride stalks even the most committed players in an organization.

PART TWO

EXECUTING
FIRST THINGS
FIRST

DEFINING THE WHO: SEE THE VISION

In the late 1970s, I had an out-of-body experience standing in the middle of Olsen Field at College Station, Texas. It was the first inning of a nine-inning game under the lights—the second half of a doubleheader between the Chaparrals of Lubbock Christian University and the Aggies of Texas A&M. I was on the mound preparing to pitch in the most important game of my career.

In my mind, it was a game of biblical proportions—a clear case of David against Goliath. The Texas A&M team was superb: a perennial NCAA Division I powerhouse. Lubbock Christian was superb, as well: a perennial NAIA contender, but smaller and limited in its depth of talent.

Any baseball coach will tell you how important it is to keep the leadoff hitter off base each inning. History is replete with examples of high-scoring rallies set in motion by a leadoff hit or, worse yet, a walk. Regrettably, I walked the first batter on four pitches.

Tim Leslie, our All-American first baseman, offered a word of encouragement. "You're OK. Get us a ground ball and we'll turn two," he said.

I walked the second batter on four pitches. Tim remained optimistic. "No sweat. Just throw strikes. We'll get them out."

I walked the third batter, but this time on five pitches, not four. The A&M batter had hit one of my fastballs about 475 feet just foul. Now the bases were loaded, and Tim was very, very quiet.

Head coach Larry Hays had seen enough. Motioning for time, Hays made his way to the mound along with Bob Nottebart, my roommate and our catcher.

"Dan, what's the problem?" Hays asked.

"I think I'm nervous," I said.

Hays did not miss a beat. "You're nervous? Think about me, I've got you pitching for me," he joked.

He got serious for a moment. "Just let these guys

hit it. *We've got seven guys standing behind you, all on full scholarship. They'll get these guys out, but you have to put the ball in play first by letting these guys just hit the ball."*

I understood what he was saying, and I knew I could throw strikes. "I'll do it, Coach," I said with confidence.

As Hays trotted back to the dugout, I turned to Nottebart. He had a concerned look on his face. "Dano," he said, "you have no stuff today. Your curveball isn't curving, your slider isn't sliding, and your fastball isn't fast."

He was right—I was going nowhere as if I had an appointment. "Notty," I said, "thanks for calming my nerves. Now, go back there and give me a big target."

Nottebart strolled back to home plate, squatted down and gave the signal for a fastball. The fourth batter for Texas A&M dug in. I fired my best pitch, and he hit a grand slam directly over the centerfield fence.

Coach Hays came out of the dugout and made his way back to the mound. "Dan," he said with a bit of a smile, "I didn't expect you to let him hit it that far." It was, by all accounts, every pitcher's nightmare.

Walt McAlexander, our team statistician and a man I admired and respected, could not contain himself. "You know, Dan," he said, "it's impossible to calculate your earned-run average if you don't get anyone out." Even I had to laugh.

As I sit here today and reflect on that experience, I am mindful not of the pain of the performance, but of the humor reflected in Coach Hays's perspective. He knew, of course, an incalculable earned-run average was not ideal, but, more important, he knew it was not the end of the world.

Following this performance and a number of others marked by a penchant for walking batters, I returned to Houston and worked on a new pitch. Returning to Lubbock the next season, I quickly sought Coach Hays.

"I learned a new pitch," I excitedly told him.

"What is it, a strike?" Hays countered.

Humor helped Hays always keep the perspective that Lubbock Christian's vision is about providing students with developmental growth in academics, spirituality, character, and leadership. Having a low earned-run average is conspicuously missing from the list. I got the loss that day against Texas A&M, but I gained something invaluable: a perspective that helped shape me into the person I am.

Vision matters. An organization's vision represents the purpose of its existence—the heart of what it is as an entity. At United, our vision is to glorify God by serving and enriching the lives of others through humility, integrity, excellence, and responsibility. Any team member reading such a statement understands United Supermarkets is all about servanthood.

Knowing and understanding the vision creates a level playing field for an organization's team members and partners. For example, it is common at United for team members at a particular store to pitch in to help coworkers. Such was the case in one store when the son of one of the managers was diagnosed with cancer.

Team members working with the manager quietly raised several thousand dollars to help the family offset the cost of medical care. The company pitched in as well, making a significant cash donation as part of a program called United We Care. The program—conceived, designed, and funded by team members—enables coworkers to assist peers in times of extraordinary need. The program is a splendid manifestation of the company's vision of serving and enriching the lives of others.

Each day, team members make decisions based largely on their knowledge of United's vision. *In culture-driven, people-centered organizations, training manuals and checklists may have a role in standardizing policies or programs, but they do not take the place of the organization's heart and soul.* A clearly communicated and understood vision statement empowers team members to make decisions that support the organization's higher purpose.

Since leaders cannot delegate responsibility, they must rely on delegating authority to get much of the work done. It is impossible to equip everyone with a list of action steps that will cover every conceivable scenario. On the other hand, it is possible to ensure that everyone in the organization understands who you are and who you aspire to be. Having this knowledge creates workplace ambassadors with a license to make good on the higher purpose.

This knowledge connects people to a common cause, resulting in a high level of trust and a degree of order, both of which are necessary in today's world. Some leaders wrestle with the concept of a vision statement, never really grasping the pervasive way in which a vision unleashes potential. This simple illustration might help leaders grasp the idea.

Every day of the year, millions upon millions of automobile drivers use the country's interstate highways to get from one place to the next. Despite the close proximity of cars traveling at a high rate of speed, a relatively small number of accidents occur. Why do you suppose this is the case?

While there are a few who are driving under the influence or who suffer a medical emergency, what keeps the highways safe is the fact that automobile drivers will do almost anything to keep from crashing into each other. In other words, all but a few drivers subscribe to the vision of self-preservation.

As a result, drivers realize a high level of trust and a degree of order every time they travel. Moreover, consider how this vision of self-preservation unleashes the potential of human beings—people go, see, and broaden their experiences because everyone embraces a common vision.

If you see the interstate highway analogy as it relates to vision, then you can also appreciate the disruption that even one driver failing to embrace it can cause. Things tend to go bad. What is compelling about a great vision well communicated is people will do almost anything to keep from compromising it.

Using the analogy again, even when bad drivers create a threat by easing over into a lane of traffic other than their own, all other drivers react instinctively. They do whatever they need to do to preserve the vision—in this case, safety—even if it means occasionally breaking the rules they were taught during driver's education.

Leaders greatly determine the extent to which people feel empowered to remain faithful to the vision. *In a culture-driven, people-centered organization, leaders celebrate actions that support the vision, even if people occasionally bend or break some rules or policies in the process.* In the context of the driving analogy, we would celebrate driver safety rather than comment on the failure to signal before changing lanes to avoid an accident.

Such is the case with organizations committed to a simple, easily remembered vision statement. Team members can make thousands of decisions with confidence because they have a license to make good on the vision, even in the absence of a supervisor telling them what to do. Frankly, standing by a strong vision statement reduces the need for a lot of language in employee handbooks and orientation checklists.

Understandably, attorneys typically drive such lists in hopes of closing loopholes and standardizing actions.

They seem to prefer long lists of do nots—"do not do this and do not do that"—which establish a negative tone from the beginning of a person's employment.

Sometimes general guidelines are necessary, but most organizations rely upon handbooks as crutches—an expedient way to dole out discipline. *In a culture-driven, people-centered organization, leaders spend more time building relationships and communicating the vision to people and less time devising ways to catch people intent on disrupting the process.*

Communicating the vision effectively allows supervisors to present disciplinary steps in the context of the higher purpose. When an issue arises with a team member, the conversation takes on a different tone. It is easy to state the obvious: "You were late. You violated rule number 23." This approach is short and to the point, but it fails to deliver a connection to the vision—the higher purpose. The only thing a team member learns from this encounter is a rule was broken, the punishment for which is "disciplinary action up to and including termination."

A people-centered approach might be to say, "Our vision here is to serve others. We hired you because we felt you bring something special to our team. If you are late, we cannot serve our guests as well as when you are here on time." The alternative approach delivers the news in the context of the vision and leaves the team member with an understanding of how unique the person's contribution to the organization is, a lasting thought that says, "I need to be on time because I bring something to the organization only I can bring."

In an organization consumed with numbers, quoting chapter and verse from the employee handbook is preferred and considered more comfortable. *In a culture-driven, people-centered organization, tying performance to successful attainment of the vision is preferred and is more comfortable for all involved.*

In the same way a vision is important to an organization, individuals need to identify a personal vision statement, as well. Too often, people drift through life, never really aspiring to anything other than surviving another day. Contrary to popular belief, the problem of drifting through life is not limited to marginalized segments of our society.

It is, in fact, quite common to see men and women who have been afforded enormous blessings in terms of education, health, and family support wandering through life with no sense of direction. Consider the simplicity of this thought. Everyone needs purpose, something that draws you out of bed rather than gets you out of bed; passion, something you pursue with all your heart; and priority, which gives you hope for the future.

Regrettably, some people decide to lock into a vision with little regard for how things might change over time. It may seem counterintuitive to think a vision statement requires changing now and then, but it is true. This is especially true if you accept a vision as the heart of the organization. Why would you change who you are? In reality, certain dramatic events can occur in life to alter who you are.

For example, recently we had a team member retire from the company after many years of service. One year prior to his retirement date, I sat down with him one-on-one to discuss a new vision for his life. He had spent so many years consumed with United's vision that he had given virtually no thought to life after United.

As I sat and listened to him, I could tell he was a person of faith and was happily married, which gave him purpose and passion. However, he really had no plans, leaving him with no priority. Sadly, he had nothing to look forward to in his life. He needed a new vision.

Organizations are not dissimilar. On some occasions, they need dramatic changes—a type of change that occurs rarely, but nonetheless can still occur. However, changing the vision just for the sake of change is a mistake organizations and individuals must avoid because it creates instability and makes convincing communication among team members and families almost impossible.

Remember, communication is one important key to success when it comes to the organization's vision. In the absence of information regarding the vision, team members will frequently assume the worst.

In Aisle 2, we discussed the psychology of gains and losses and the finding that there is greater fear of loss than desire for gain. This is particularly true in Western culture because ego plays such an important part in our self-esteem. Most people are consumed with fear of failure but are unwilling to openly acknowledge it. The reason: it is all about ego. Business leaders capable of exchanging their ego for humility are more likely to see upside potential and gains than people who are imprisoned by fear.

Many business leaders will not seek opportunities that require risk because they do not want to fail and suffer a hit to their egos.

Think you are exempt?

Try this experiment sometime anywhere but in Las Vegas. Ask a stranger to accept this hypothetical gamble: you will flip a coin, and if the coin lands on heads, you will pay the person $1,000, and if the coin lands on tails, the person will pay you $1,000. Almost without exception, people will decline the offer because the pain of losing $1,000 is greater than the pleasure of gaining $1,000.

Again, using Drs. Tversky and Kahneman's model, you can see how the S curve in the graph plots the subjective (pain or pleasure) with the objective (the $1,000 amount). Most people fear losing more than anything. Failure to keep people informed leads to fear, the second-biggest obstacle to successful vision attainment. (The first is pride, which we will discuss later in the book.)

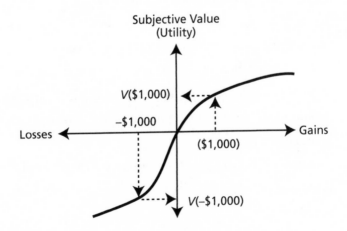

Leaders must never grow tired of talking or modeling their vision. They may change it from time to time, but they must constantly remind their followers of the vision because it represents the heart of the organization.

Many challenges will confront an organization, a family, or an individual over time, but having a vision keeps things in perspective. In the same way that no one has ever sustained life without a heart, organizations, families, and individuals must identify who they really are as they establish their vision or forfeit sustained success.

Culture-driven, people-centered organizations start with the vision because it represents a stable platform, an anchor in a sea of change. Experts will differ regarding the most effective way to develop the vision, but answering these few questions is all it takes. Here are some tips and questions for developing a meaningful vision.

First, think big. For organizations, ask the stakeholders to share ideas regarding the need for the organization's existence. Ensure the emphasis is on culture and people.

Second, identify what sustainable difference the organization will make for humankind that will transcend time.

Third, focus on the vitals—those deep-seated values the team is unwilling to compromise. Most leaders find the vision reflects above all a heart and soul.

One final tip worth remembering: keep the vision short, very short. Long vision statements are hard to recall and get lost over time. Less is more when it comes to articulating who you are.

To illustratre brevity in vision statements, I list just a few of my favorites delivered by recognizable organizations and individuals. Note how each statement incorporates a higher purpose.

"We bring good things to life."

GENERAL ELECTRIC

"We know what it means to serve."

USAA, A COMPANY SERVING MILITARY

MEMBERS AND THEIR FAMILIES

"We must motivate ourselves to do our very best, and by our example lead others to do their best as well."

TRUETT CATHY, CHICK-FIL-A

"Take a journey you will always remember."

HARLEY-DAVIDSON

"We hold these truths to be self-evident,
that all men are created equal."
THOMAS JEFFERSON'S VISION FOR
THE AMERICAN PHILOSOPHY OF FREEDOM

"India will be free; you are merely guests in our land."
MAHATMA GANDHI'S VISION FOR REMOVING THE BRITISH,
CREATING AN INDEPENDENT INDIA

For personal vision statements, a quick way to get started is to write your own obituary, first reflecting your current circumstances and then reflecting who you aspire to be down the road. The exercise is good because it forces you to take a different perspective. An effective vision statement has less to do with success and more to do with significance.

In other words, "Increase return on assets by 4 percent" is not a vision statement, although numbers-oriented organizations believe and communicate that these statements move people to do their best. A more appropriate vision for a culture-driven, people-centered organization with the same desire might be, "Improve as many lives as possible."

Improving the lives of as many people as possible may warrant leveraging capital to build more stores so the organization can interact with more people. Such a plan would most likely increase the return on assets, but for reasons more noble than the number itself. More important, the vision positions the organization for sustained success in an area of significance.

In the same way everything rises and falls as a result of leadership, leadership rises and falls as a result of a clear vision, effortlessly communicated and easily understood. When it comes to the importance of vision, perhaps the inspired writer of Proverbs said it best, "Where there is no vision, the people perish."

FROM THE EXPRESS LANE

- ❊ An organization's vision represents the purpose for its existence.

- ❊ Leaders must spend more time communicating the vision to people and less time devising ways to catch people intent on disrupting the process.

- ❊ A vision statement must be changed and updated when necessary.

- ❊ Failure to keep people informed leads to fear, the second-biggest obstacle to successful vision attainment.

- ❊ An effective vision statement has more to do with significance than with success.

DEFINING THE WHAT: KNOW THE MISSION

Defining what you are doing to realize your vision brings clarity to an organization. Shortly after I joined the leadership ranks at United, we decided to rework our mission statement. By the standards of most companies, our existing mission statement was short (35 words), but none of us on the executive team could recall it, which meant we could not expect thousands of team members to remember it either.

We needed fewer words. We needed a short statement that best described what we were trying to accomplish at United Supermarkets. In short, we needed a powerful call to action we could all remember—words that would breathe life into our vision of serving and enriching the lives of others.

Our team was inspired to take action after watching a documentary on the National Aeronautics and Space Administration, better known as NASA. The film highlighted what was arguably the most publicized mission statement in the world in the 1960s. President John F. Kennedy challenged the nation to land a man on the moon and return him safely by the end of the decade. That challenge, made in 1961, meant the fledgling space program had to marshal all of its resources with great speed.

To aid the team's focus, NASA's leaders issued a new mission statement that matched the organization's new vision: "Perform manned lunar landing and return safely," which was shortened by many at NASA to, "The Moon."

Despite NASA's lack of specific focus since its inception in 1958, its mission statement in the 1960s inspired extraordinary accomplishments unlike anything before. Historians who interviewed many people at NASA at the time remarked that everyone seemed unusually focused on the mission. From janitors to rocket scientists, the singularly focused team at NASA seemed extraordinarily confident. Failure was not an option.

While the people at United did not change the course of world history by sending a man to the moon, our new mission statement did transform our company's history. Our revised mission statement contained six words:

Ultimate Service

Superior Performance

Positive Impact

T HESE HALF-DOZEN WORDS changed the way our stakeholders looked at the business.

More important, team members at every position in the company chose to embrace the words, commit them to memory, and bring them to life. Today, we expect every team member working at United to comprehend the mission statement and its importance to daily operations.

Many organizations feel compelled to write a mission statement, but often they tuck those critical words away in a binder and place it on a shelf. Not surprisingly, they fail to tap into the tremendous power reserves that would be at their disposal if they just succinctly stated the organization's commitment to fulfilling the vision. *Only by making the mission statement known can organizations realize their potential.*

At United, the mission statement is posted everywhere—in meeting rooms, offices, stores, and even store break rooms. Additionally, whenever possible, team members are encouraged to sign the posters in their own hand—a simple way of ensuring personal ownership and individual accountability. Clearly, the most convincing evidence that a mission statement exists is to model it every day.

Mission statements eliminate the confusion inherent in large organizations. Day after day, a mission statement reminds everyone in the organization of the expectations. It is the equivalent of calibrating the organization frequently, which provides everyone with a common view of our responsibilities.

Once an organization embraces this discipline, it can deal with adversity much more effectively because team members instinctively seek to accomplish the mission—they understand the language. Even when a crisis or unforeseen circumstance dictates changing the mission, proper discipline minimizes the negative impact on an organization.

For example, NASA launched Apollo 13 from Kennedy Space Center in Florida on April 11, 1970.

Astronauts James Lovell, John Swigert, and Fred Haise were planning to carry out a specific mission: a precision lunar landing in the Fra Mauro highlands on the moon, surveying and sampling the Imbrium Basin, and deploying and activating the Apollo Lunar Surface Experiments Package.

In addition, the Apollo team planned to further develop the capability to work in the lunar environment and photograph candidate exploration sites. All of NASA's team understood Apollo 13's deliverables; they had trained and prepared for years specifically to execute the mission.

Two days after launch, an onboard explosion placed the astronauts in peril. The crew made radio contact with Mission Control using a phrase most of us have come to know: "Houston, we've had a problem." The Service Module was losing oxygen and electric power, forcing the three astronauts to use the Lunar Module as a temporary "lifeboat" while NASA engineers worked feverishly to devise a solution to save their lives.

In 1995, Ron Howard directed the motion picture *Apollo 13*, a riveting account of the events surrounding the safe recovery of the astronauts. In one of the film's many compelling scenes, the dramatization shows a team of ingenious flight controllers working shoulder to shoulder in a cramped room to develop an innovative solution for the crew's safe return to Earth.

The scene portrays tension, frustration, and chaos—sheer panic seizes the team, all of whom are professionals with a preference for the order and stability found in math and science. Amid the confusion is a growing sense of urgency and a fear of losing the three astronauts.

In the film, flight director Gene Kranz, portrayed by Ed Harris, walks into the room, picks up a piece of chalk and draws two circles on the blackboard, one representing the Earth and one representing the moon. He draws the trajectory of Apollo 13, clearly illustrating the gap between the current flight path and the one necessary for safe recovery of the astronauts. The room becomes quiet.

Kranz proceeds to establish NASA's new mission statement for Apollo 13, safe recovery, and, in doing so, promptly ends talk of losing the astronauts. Without hesitation, the flight controllers recalibrate their thinking, restore order, and begin focusing on the new mission of Apollo 13. Using makeshift parts and equipment assembled by the astronauts, NASA's team delivers a successful solution just in time to save the astronauts' lives.

Apollo 13 returned safely on April 17, 1970, having failed to accomplish what the team had initially set out to do. Even so, in his own appearances and writings after the mission, Lovell referred to Apollo 13 as "a successful failure," opting to emphasize NASA's successful attainment of what became a more important mission for the people-centered organization: the safe recovery of three human beings.

The story is one of leadership, teamwork, imagination, and persistence—qualities that benefit any organization. It would not surprise many people to learn NASA was a culture-driven organization during its infancy. Not unlike the military, NASA built its organization on a "mission accomplishment" culture, one that was committed to achieving specific objectives and goals; however, NASA had something more: a people-centeredness lacking in most organizations.

In the case of Apollo 13, the organization allowed its people to deliver the lifesaving solutions because its leaders had created an environment of constantly cultivating great ideas and superior performance.

An organization needs both a mission-oriented culture and a high regard for people. Critics often suggest a culture can be mission-oriented or people-oriented, but not both. They claim mission-oriented cultures stringently pursue specified goals, whereas people-oriented cultures allow workforce flexibility, which places the two at odds. Sadly, such thinking leads organizations to believe they have little choice. They resign themselves to being one or the other and develop their entire mission around that resignation.

My view is radically different.

Since I live in an area known for agriculture, I associate the word *culture* with *cultivate*. Farmers start with nothing more than prairie; they cultivate the land and prepare the soil for seed, which ultimately delivers a harvest. While it is affected by government allotments or quotas, the type of crop planted basically centers on the person doing the planting—it is the farmer's choice. Depending on personal interest and market conditions, farmers will plant a variety of crops in the same soil on the same land that once was prairie.

The soil may lend itself to one type of crop or another, but it is the farmer who decides what the crop will be, not the prairie. The farm is culture-driven and people-centered. Its ultimate success requires the constant cultivation of the seed chosen. It is a proven, sustainable model employed by farmers for centuries.

Sustainable organizations are much the same. They have a clear idea of what they want to grow (vision), and they rely on people empowered to choose what kind of seed to plant (mission), understanding that success will depend on the cultivation (culture) of the seed. Hence, they are culture-driven (constantly cultivating) and people-centered (embracing human beings who have a choice).

Therefore, organizations can be mission-oriented and people-oriented if the leadership is willing to devote the time necessary to create an environment in which both can blossom.

117

One of my heroes is a master of blending what may seem like opposing ideas into synergistic, powerful results. Dr. Kenneth Cooper, a revolutionary in the good sense, is founder, president, and CEO of the Cooper Aerobics Center. Dr. Cooper started a worldwide fitness revolution when he published his best-selling book *Aerobics* in 1968.

Dr. Cooper has advocated revolutionizing the field of medicine, moving away from disease treatment and toward disease prevention through aerobic exercise. Visiting the Cooper Clinic, one quickly realizes it is unlike any other medical facility in the world. The antithesis of most hospital-like institutions, which often are cold and impersonal, the clinic is warm, inviting, and peaceful. The emphasis from the start of a patient's appointment is one of prevention, not confrontation. Today, thousands of people trek to this unique clinic for annual fitness exams.

Why do you suppose people would go to the trouble of scheduling a comprehensive fitness exam months in advance that requires travel across the country?

Dr. Cooper's mission is to provide patients with the tools, education, and motivation to live a healthy and active lifestyle. As a result, his team members are committed to fostering a positive environment, one focused on a brighter future characterized by prevention, fitness, and wellness.

The Cooper Clinic is a wonderful example of a culture-driven, people-centered organization, but it did not get that way by accident. Every doctor, nurse, and administrator understands the clinic's mission statement because the disciplined team acts in a manner supportive of the higher purpose: Dr. Cooper's singular vision. Patients sense this commitment and experience the difference.

In the absence of a disciplined approach to mission accomplishment, organizations tend to wander, never really focusing on specifics. Ironically, advertising agencies, which routinely assist leaders in developing mission statements, are among the worst at following their own advice.

Many are drawn by the allure of winning awards or capturing accounts and, as a result, they never fully deliver on the claims that they build brands and drive sales. It would be easy to suggest that creative people do not understand businesspeople and vice versa, but this would not be true. They understand each other, but they are often pursuing different missions. These critical remarks are based on my own experience. Before returning to United, I was one of the principals in an advertising organization.

For a number of years, it seemed our advertising company was struggling to focus on what we did differently from competing companies. Despite the fact we often helped clients develop their own vision and mission statements, we seemed oblivious to our own need for direction. At one point, we became too consumed with assessing our competition, constantly worrying about what "they" were developing behind the scenes. Finally, one day my business partner and the company founder introduced the team to a new word advanced in Edward de Bono's book *Sur/Petition.*

119

According to de Bono, obsessing over competition, with its focus on what others are doing, is just a baseline for survival. Sur/Petition, on the other hand, focuses on value creation, going beyond traditional strategic competition to exploit the potential of integrated values.

Being introduced to de Bono's work proved invaluable to our team. We quickly became less interested in everyone else and more focused on what value we could bring to clients. We identified a mission statement that clearly outlined our deliverables in a way clients could appreciate:.

- Increase relevancy
- Collapse time to market
- Improve return on investment

Almost immediately, the new mission statement changed the organization. From that day on, all decisions regarding new products or services had to pass the mission statement test. In other words, our team agreed if a new product or a new service could not increase the relevancy of the advertising, collapse the time to market for promotional material, or improve a client's return on investment in advertising, we would not spend time pursuing it.

The sense of direction brought about by our mission statement was clarifying, but it was also much more than that—it was liberating. Everyone in the organization felt a renewed commitment to advance our cause for clients. No longer did our brochures and other collateral material sound stale, overwritten, and out of touch with the markets. Materials now contained precise language written to make our products easily identifiable and easily purchased.

The hardest part of embracing the newly developed mission statement was learning to say no. This is true of all organizations seriously committed to bringing mission statements to life. It forces people in the organization to come to grips with what they knew to be true all along—we cannot please everyone, and we cannot be stellar at everything. Remaining faithful to the vision and the mission, even if it means passing on an acquisition or electing not to develop a new product requested by a client, is what matters most. It could mean resigning some accounts from time to time.

Organizations serious about their mission statements must reshape what they are busy doing every day to ensure the effort is synchronized with what they plan to deliver.

At United, we completely reshaped our understanding of what ultimate service meant to our guests.
We challenged our thinking by going outside our
industry to identify best practices. Additionally, we
recruited guests to serve on Guest Advisory Boards,
forums for exchanging information directly with our
guests regarding what was important in the area of
service.

Next, we examined each store in the chain to determine steps needed to enhance performance. In the
spirit of searching for superior performance, even
stores with commendable performance got a hard
look. Our team members provided feedback regarding areas of waste and inefficiency. Together, our team
embarked on a steady drive toward a new performance standard. We abandoned practices that were
more self-serving than beneficial to our guests.

For example, we stopped requiring canned goods
to be perfectly aligned on shelves when we came to
terms with the reality that we were operating grocery
stores, not museums. United realized a dramatic savings from this one minor change, even though it was
difficult to implement because it represented a
decades-old practice.

Finally, we reviewed our efforts to make a positive impact in the communities we served. We looked at everything from monetary and product donations to more time-intensive participation in community service projects in an effort to improve our standing in each trade area. Rather than rest on our previous accomplishments, we opted to embrace changes when and where possible and practical.

Sometimes change meant deconstructing something that had worked for a long time but no longer seemed effective. We struggled with the process of dismantling existing programs to build new programs, recognizing the investment in money and time necessary for sustainability. Our struggle improved the organization and brought about a spirit of collaboration not fully experienced previously.

As a result, we discovered what all culture-driven, people-centered organizations find to be true about any good mission statement: the inspiration creates a wonderful journey. It is more a direction than a destination, one that moves the organization closer to realizing the vision, closer to becoming what it wants to be.

FROM THE EXPRESS LANE

❈ A powerful, short mission statement brings clarity to your organization.

❈ The mission statement must be consistently communicated throughout the organization or it and the organization will gather dust.

❈ An organization needs both a mission-oriented and a people-oriented culture. The two must coexist and complement each other.

❈ A clear mission statement allows the people in an organization to realize it is impossible to please everyone or be stellar at everything.

DEFINING THE WHEN: KEEP THE FAITH

The first time I met Jim "Mattress Mack" McIngvale, he sold my wife a new bed and gave me a basketball for tagging along. The consummate merchant, McIngvale is a local celebrity and the owner of Gallery Furniture in Houston, Texas. In addition to offering reasonably priced furnishings, Gallery Furniture pays tribute to many of McIngvale's personal interests. His predilection for cars, sports, movie stars, and pop-culture icons makes McIngvale one of the more interesting people you will meet.

Gallery Furniture enjoys remarkable success. A two-warehouse complex located on Interstate 45 just north of Houston, Gallery embodies its owner's *passion for fun. McIngvale is at his best in front of people. An unlimited source of energy keeps him in constant motion. McIngvale can outsell any salesperson on the face of the earth and still have time to hand out basketballs in the parking lot. His success stems, in part, from two promises to customers.*

Promise No. 1: "I'll save you money."
Promise No. 2: "Buy it today; get it today."

Unlike other furniture retailers, Gallery Furniture delivers purchases the same day they are made. Buy a big-screen television in the morning, and the odds are good you will watch the big game on it at home that afternoon. As a result, people flock to Gallery to satisfy the need for instant gratification. Gallery Furniture makes good on a statement one of my furniture clients was fond of making when asked about best sellers. "The best sellers," he would say, "are the items we have in stock." He was right. Most people do not want to wait months for a piece of furniture.

The day my wife took me to Gallery Furniture, we spotted some nice beds, but we did not find exactly what we had in mind. We left the store, got in the car, and started to pull out of the parking lot. Much to my surprise, a man came out of the store and motioned for us to stop. It was "Mattress Mack" himself. I rolled down my window. McIngvale pleaded with us to return to the store. "I'll make you a great deal on a bed you're going to love!"

I explained our predicament, but McIngvale insisted we return. By now, other customers were forming a crowd around the celebrity furniture salesman. I parked the car, and we went back inside. We bought a new bed, saved 80 dollars, and left with a basketball for my son. The bed was delivered that afternoon.

127

It all happened so fast. My wife and I still laugh about the incident.

In his autobiography, Always Think Big, *McIngvale confesses:*

"People respond to actions far more readily than they do to words. For example, when I'm right there in front of people acting on delighting customers, my employees can see and feel my commitment and my passion. It's much harder to convey that emotion in words. . . . I could be like other business owners and leave the work of selling and customer service to

others. I don't because I believe that a leader must be present."

McIngvale knew the truth: Gallery Furniture is what it is because Jim McIngvale is who he is. The person and the enterprise are interdependent. Without "Mattress Mack" in the store, Gallery Furniture would be a different experience. Not necessarily a bad experience, but different nonetheless. McIngvale chose not to develop additional locations because he wanted to remain faithful to the experience that only he could offer. Many organizations, especially publicly traded companies, succumb to the pressure for growth, ultimately compromising both their vision and their mission—who they are and what they do.

128

D IFFERENT COMPANIES HAVE different reasons for growth. Regrettably, too many pursue growth without regard for consequences. For example, one of the more popular reasons for growth nowadays seems to be to mask a lack of performance. Given the pressure applied by shareholders and financial analysts on underperforming publicly traded companies, acquisitions have become popular and convenient. This might buy time while due diligence and other activities are conducted, but it rarely addresses the root problem.

Growth can have other, less sinister, temptations for companies.

Right after the turn of the century, United embarked upon an aggressive growth plan that nearly crippled our company on three strategic fronts. We made poor real estate decisions, overbuilt facilities, and outpaced our ability to provide the necessary talent to ensure success. It was a sobering example of a company straying from its core principles. Our leadership team and our financial advisers believed we had a superior strategy. We were all swept away by a wave of excitement and did not remain faithful to the mission of ultimate service, superior performance, and positive impact.

As a result, the morale of team members suffered. Performance deteriorated as well. A number of senior team members departed during this challenging time in our history. The company's growth plan was suspended indefinitely. Not surprisingly, some of our strongest critics were those who had been so enthusiastic about the growth plan and had encouraged it in the first place.

To restore financial stability and a spirit of hope among our team members, a painfully comprehensive restructuring of the company required the first layoffs in 87 years. This was more than looking over spreadsheets and selecting names; it was an emotionally exhausting experience that involved sleepless nights and second thoughts. It was also among the lowest points in United's history because of the damage done to the trust levels among the company's family owners, senior leaders, team members, and guests.

Sadly, our company, built on the premise that people are its heart and soul, had failed on this most basic tenet.

Despite this setback, the company emerged more "United" than ever before, and it took less than a year because of unwavering faithfulness to the principles upon which the company was founded. *At the heart of the turnaround, however, was open, honest communication about the mistakes that had been made and about what it would take to erase those errors.* I am convinced the turnaround would not have happened so quickly and would not have been so successful without a strong commitment to open communication.

United, of course, is not alone. Many other organizations stray from their vision and mission, enticed by the prospect of wealth or unaware of their own limited capacity to execute. Krispy Kreme's brand started with founder Vernon Rudolph. Over time, the family-owned company expanded throughout the southeast, but the pace of expansion was slow and measured—a direct result of Rudolph's commitment to quality.

In 1973, the founder died, and the company was sold several times. Krispy Kreme went public in 2000 in an effort to aid its growth. On opening day, the stock took off and increased in value to about $37, four times the opening price. Not long after Krispy Kreme went public, things began to change.

Instead of driving sales through reinvestment in individual stores, Krispy Kreme reportedly focused on growing revenues and profits at the parent company by forcing its franchisees to purchase equipment and ingredients from headquarters at significantly marked-up prices. At the same time, Krispy Kreme sought to maximize royalty payments by adding outlets in crowded markets, forcing franchisees to compete with each other.

Finally, Krispy Kreme began an aggressive whole-sale venture, selling products through satellite locations such as supermarkets, gas stations, and kiosks. Krispy Kreme became ubiquitous, diluted, and less appealing because its growth meant compromising the product and the experience.

Not surprisingly, quality suffered and unit sales slumped. Suddenly, shareholders lost their taste for Krispy Kreme, and the stock price plummeted. By September 2006, the *Wall Street Journal* reported the company was unable to file a full second-quarter financial report with federal regulators because of prior "material weaknesses" in its bookkeeping. The tragedy rests with the leaders of the organization.

One of those leaders, former Krispy Kreme executive vice president Jack McAleer, is doing his part to derive something good from the experience. McAleer shared some insightful remarks during a speech delivered to students attending Benedictine College in Atchison, Kansas, in September 2006. In discussing Krispy Kreme's storied history, its meteoric rise to the top in the 1990s, and its more recent plunge into legal and financial difficulties, McAleer was quoted:

> Don't get sucked into the world. We were a darling of Wall Street, the media, and the public. You can imagine the money, power, and notoriety. Those are things that can lead to sin. You can imagine riding that wave. It was easy to get

caught up in everything. We began losing sight of our vocation. We were spending more time working than with our families. It can happen so easily. Don't lose sight of what's important. No matter what your career path is, don't lose sight of God.

Similarly, Boston Market, formerly Boston Chicken, is another prime example. The chain grew from 20 stores in the late 1980s to more than 900 stores by 1998. The infrastructure costs at the chain outpaced the sales generated by its individual stores—the company could not pay its bills or repay its loans. The chain filed for Chapter 11 bankruptcy protection in 1998 and proceeded to close nearly 200 stores. McDonald's bought the chain in 2000, largely for what appears to be its prime real estate locations, not the restaurant concept.

Of course, franchised organizations are not the only examples of destructive growth. May Company attempted to grow through a series of failed acquisitions, only to concede defeat, sell to Federated Department Stores, and leave the retail industry. Kmart lost its way and embraced an offer by Sears to bail the troubled retailer out of bankruptcy. Albertson's proved that even a Jack Welch–trained executive could not stem the tide of steadily declining earnings. A consortium of companies, including Supervalu, now owns the chain.

In each of these examples, the failure rests not with the organization's people, but with its leaders. It is the leaders, not the front-line team members, who embark on overly aggressive growth plans involving risky acquisitions and unrealistic execution expectations. Too often, such plans fail miserably because the projected synergies are never realized and shareholder value is destroyed.

134

The facts speak for themselves. In September 2002, the magazine *Fast Company* printed an article entitled, "Size Is Not a Strategy." The article summarized the amount of value destroyed in the ten biggest mergers since 1998. First on the list was the AOL–Time Warner merger consummated in 2001. By the summer of 2002, shareholders had seen a whopping $148 million in value destroyed.

In fact, of the ten largest consummated transactions, only one, the merger of Travelers and Citicorp in 1998, created value. The remaining nine megamergers cost shareholders nearly $800 billion in value. New accounting rules resulted in about $1 trillion in corporate writedowns, or reductions, in the book value of investments in the first quarter of 2002.

While there may be no single reason for an organization's failure to grow properly or the destruction of value brought about by a merger, *the lack of faithfulness to the original vision and the mission consistently destroys sustained success*. Organizations stop talking about who they are or what they do that separates them from the pack. Instead, they begin talking about synergies and efficiencies, which in theory is not a bad thing, but it is not what leads to sustainability.

Growth is a good thing, but not at the expense of the unique values that define the organization.

At United, we have a distinguished 90-year history that reminds us daily we are a company that is built to serve others. Yes, we have a desire for growth, but these days we work extra hard to remain grounded in the process and faithful to our vision, especially after our own painful experience.

Because Ultimate Service is a cornerstone of our organization, we understand staffing is the single largest obstacle to rapid expansion. Since we insist on remaining faithful to our vision and our mission, the pace of our growth is established largely by our ability to recruit, train, and retain talented team

135

members who know what it means to render Ultimate Service.

Not surprisingly, bankers and investors are eager these days to fund the construction of 25, 50, or even 100 stores on our behalf. They want us to grow the chain rapidly, spreading expenses over the stores, realizing economies of scale, and enhancing profitability through the efficiencies gained by operating more units. As a privately held, family-owned company, we routinely decline such requests if building a new store would compromise our vision and our mission. As a result, our growth will vary—some years we may add one store, and some years we may add five stores. Regardless, every store we build will reflect faithfulness to the principles on which the company was founded.

Privately held companies that are not family-owned understand the challenges their publicly traded counterparts face. Quite often, the challenges are no different. It is the same dilemma: they must grow, but they must also perform at the level their investors expect. Starbucks experienced this dilemma in the years immediately following Howard Schultz's purchase of the company from its original founders.

In a detailed Starbucks case study, written by Arthur Thompson and John Gamble for the book

Strategic Management, the authors summarize the struggles inherent in attempting to satisfy growth and performance goals.

Central to the company's story is the fact that the Starbucks experience was not built overnight. It took patience. It took foresight. It took Schultz's conviction and principles to convince investors to wait and reap long-term benefits from the power of the brand, even in the face of early losses. Patient investors may seem like an oxymoron these days, but sometimes patience, not unrelenting pressure, is what is needed. Starbucks benefited from its farsightedness because its leader met personally with all of the financial investors.

Even today, Schultz tempers his appetite for growth with the understanding that patience and faithfulness to the Starbucks experience is imperative, regardless of what investors or analysts desire. In early 2007, an internal memo written by Schultz to his staff entitled "The Commoditization of the Starbucks Experience" appeared in the *Wall Street Journal*.

In his memo, Schultz wrote in part:

Over the past ten years, in order to achieve the growth, development, and scale necessary to go from less than 1,000 stores to 13,000 stores and beyond, we have had to make a series of decisions that, in retrospect, have led to the watering down of the Starbucks experience, and, what some might call, the commoditization of our brand. Many of these decisions were probably right at the time, and on their own merit would not have created the dilution of the experience; but in this case, the sum is much greater and, unfortunately, much more damaging than the original pieces.

Schultz's memo serves as a poignant reminder that publicly traded companies often become too preoccupied with satisfying Wall Street; they become slaves to faceless investors and financial analysts. In the absence of strong leadership with strong convictions, such organizations begin a perilous journey toward moral bankruptcy and ultimate failure.

It does not have to be this way. *All companies are capable of growing while remaining faithful to the principles that created their success in the first place, but the purpose for the growth must be sound.* If it is purely a matter of financial gain, the organization will fail to recognize the higher purpose of serving and enriching the lives of others—making a sustainable difference in the world.

Two kinds of people populate business: people who create money, and people who make money. The people who create money are visionaries who have an impact on the economy in the form of jobs, careers, and lives. They are risk takers, and they are indispensable. By contrast, the people who make money invest in the ideas that have been created by others. It should come as no surprise that there are far more investors than creators.

Investors participate in the game; creators are the game.

Jon M. Huntsman is the chairman and founder of Huntsman Corporation, a family-owned petrochemical company based in Salt Lake City, Utah, that grew to $12 billion in annual sales by the turn of the century—the largest family-owned company in the world. Huntsman took the company public in 2005, but not because he needed the infusion of capital to grow his company. He did it in large part to generate additional funds for the fight against cancer—a disease that threatened his life.

Huntsman contributed nearly a quarter of a billion dollars of his personal funds to build a cancer research institute with an accompanying research hospital; together, they represent a wellspring of hope for millions of cancer victims. Huntsman is a creator who has spent his life cultivating ways to have a positive effect on humanity.

Sheer size does not guarantee sustainability anymore, if it ever did. I have not yet turned 50, and I have witnessed firsthand the demise of too many great companies. As a child, I recall marveling at the "cathedral of commerce," the Woolworth Building in New York City, where the Woolworth company was based until it declared bankruptcy in 1997.

I recall those special days in the 1960s riding in the car with my mother to the Montgomery Ward catalog pickup point, where customers pulled up alongside phones with speakers located in the parking lot, similar to those found at drive-in movie theaters. I can still remember the excitement of using the phone to arrange for the pickup. Sadly, Montgomery Ward now is nothing more than a bygone retailing relic. Who would have imagined?

Then there was Texaco. I can still recall the Texaco jingle, "You can trust your car to the man who wears the star—the big, bright Texaco star." Like Woolworth and Montgomery Ward, the Texaco brand has all but disappeared. I feel certain someone has compiled a compendium of such historical examples, but it might be more important to wonder: who will be next?

Culture-driven, people-centered organizations remain faithful to their vision and their mission. They stiff-arm the constant pressure to compromise who they are and what they do. As a result, their growth is controlled, but their reasons for success remain unassailable. Because their model is sustainable, their future is bright. They may not make the most money or pay the highest dividend, but such organizations will return something greater, something aligned with a higher purpose of enriching the lives of others—a moral return on investment and a healthier financial standing.

141

This is good.

FROM THE EXPRESS LANE

❈ Culture-driven, people-centered organizations grow for one reason—to enrich the lives of others.

❈ The organization's leaders define and shape the experience for others.

❈ An organization must control and pace its growth or risk compromising its mission and vision.

❈ Growth is a good thing, but not at the expense of an organization's unique value system.

❈ Companies should grow with an eye on maintaining the principles that allowed them to be successful in the first place.

❈ Two kinds of people populate business: those who create and those who invest. Know the difference.

WHEN THINGS GO BAD (AND THEY WILL)

At no time is an organization's sustainability more important than when bad things happen. Sometimes the pain is self-inflicted, and other times external forces deliver the blow; either way, a culture-driven, people-centered work environment allows organizations to persevere and individuals to rebuild their lives—even when the organization is as big as the federal government and the individual is as important as the U.S. president.

Burglars broke into a plush Watergate hotel suite on June 17, 1972, in an attempt to steal files from the Democratic Party's National Committee. By 1973, an investigation had implicated Richard M. Nixon, the nation's thirty-seventh president, in

criminal and cover-up charges, setting in motion a
series of events that would have profound
consequences for the United States.

From 1973 until his resignation in August 1974,
Nixon made three major speeches on the Watergate
scandal. In the beginning, he denied any
involvement, opting to terminate the employment of
key staff members in hopes of avoiding painful
impeachment proceedings. Eventually, Nixon
succumbed to pressure and resigned during a speech
televised around the world.

I was 15 years old, and, like virtually all
Americans, I was consumed with the ordeal. The
thought of the most powerful man in the free world
resigning from office and facing criminal prosecution
left me confused and disappointed. President Gerald
Ford, Nixon's successor, referred to the ordeal as a
"national nightmare." Despite a presidential pardon
from Ford, Nixon left office a national disgrace amid
lingering controversy.

Certainly, this was a dark period in U.S. history,
but the most compelling event for me took place just
minutes before Nixon left the White House. In a
moving and impromptu speech to cabinet members,
friends, and White House staff, Nixon reflected on

the events that led to his demise. I was particularly interested in Nixon's comments because the circumstances were so odd, so self-inflicted. I wondered what he could say to heal the hearts of his most trusted staff members and friends.

He said a great deal in fewer than 2,000 words. In addition to thanking the team of people gathered to say good-bye, Nixon acknowledged their service and expressed his hope that the events surrounding the Watergate scandal would not dissuade young people from politics or government service. He shared a brief story of perseverance taken from the life of former U.S. President Theodore Roosevelt, and he reflected on matters of a purpose higher than politics.

As he spoke, Nixon became understandably emotional. He reflected on his parents, their example, and his love for his family. Finally, he spoke of God, humility, faith, and prayer.

S INCE THAT DAY, I have read and reread Nixon's final comments many times. Without making any political judgments regarding his professional performance, Nixon's last speech represented a humbling and clear look into the soul of a human being, reveal-

ing two things common to all of us: first, things sometimes go bad in organizations, and second, individual
healing begins where pride ends.

Regrouping when things go bad is a fact of life for
all organizations. One example of successful
regrouping is just now beginning to emerge. Now,
nearly 35 years after the Watergate scandal, historians are talking about a more uplifting story—the one
about Nixon's successor, Gerald Ford, and his coura-
geous leadership in restoring the nation's trust in
government.

Gerald Ford is the only man to serve as both U.S.
vice president and U.S. president without having been
elected to office. Ford, a long-time congressional rep-
resentative from Michigan, was appointed vice president in 1973 when Spiro Agnew pleaded no contest
to tax-evasion charges. Within a year, Ford ascended
to the presidency following Nixon's resignation.

Ford entered office under extraordinarily difficult
circumstances. Historians are only just now beginning
to look at Ford's presidency in context. Many of the
decisions that Ford made while president were unpop-
ular, beginning with his pardon of Nixon. His actions,
however, make great lessons on regrouping when
things go bad. The first lesson is straightforward but

easier said than done: *make decisions based on principles, not popularity.*

Many of Ford's emotionally draining decisions may have cost him a second term, but they were all principle-based and helped the nation heal, restoring trust and a sense of normalcy. Consider just a few of the issues and Ford's corresponding decisions.

Issue 1: Watergate aftermath.

Principle applied: Do not allow past failures to hinder tomorrow's successes.

Corresponding decision: Pardon Nixon and end the national trauma.

Issue 2: Timing of the withdrawal from South Vietnam.

Principle applied: Preserve trust by honoring one's commitments.

Corresponding decision: Delay the withdrawal and evacuate as many Vietnamese as possible.

Issue 3: Global instability.

Principle applied: All human beings possess inalienable rights.

Corresponding decision: Sign the Helsinki Final Act, linking peace and security while embracing human rights.

Together, these three principles represent Ford's commitment to a higher purpose, and they remind us that personal spirituality has a place in secular society. Ford's personal faith represents the second lesson in regrouping when things go bad: *make decisions based on a godly perspective, not a worldly perspective.* A leader who makes decisions based on a godly perspective promotes selflessness and most often will do the right thing, whereas a leader who makes decisions based on a worldly perspective promotes selfishness and most often will do the most expedient thing.

148

Contrary to what secularists say, I believe leaders (particularly leaders in culture-driven, people-centered organizations) cannot separate the affairs of this world from their personal spirituality. They are inseparable, connected in a way that shapes character and dictates actions.

American history is rife with examples of how the nation's leaders sought guidance from God. The words "In God We Trust" are more than a national motto on American currency; they represent a deliberate and constant reminder of God's sovereignty.

Not unlike Ford, America's sixteenth president, Abraham Lincoln, also subscribed to a higher purpose. Despite bitter opposition from his own countrymen,

Lincoln's reliance on godly values helped him lead America to a greater understanding of freedom. The bloody Civil War, which marked his presidency, sharply divided the nation. Even so, Lincoln inspired the reunion of the country by altering the context of the war from one of blame to one of humility. Even today, his proclamation recorded in 1863 still resonates.

Lincoln wrote:

> We have been the recipients of the choicest boun-ties of Heaven. . . . We have grown in numbers, wealth and power as no other nation has ever grown. But we have forgotten God. We have for-gotten the gracious hand which preserved us in peace, and multiplied and enriched and strength-ened us; and we have vainly imagined, in the deceitfulness of our hearts, that all these blessings were produced by some superior wisdom and virtue of our own. Intoxicated with unbroken success, we have become too self-sufficient to feel the necessity of redeeming and preserving grace, too proud to pray to the God that made us!

When it comes to our professed reliance on God, Lincoln's words, written to an audience divided by civil war, suggest that not much has changed in society since 1863. This is why it is so important for leaders to start cultivating a different future. Culture-driven, people-centered organizations surrender their pride and humbly seek to honor God. Their leaders are energized and equipped to motivate followers to see beyond the present.

In short, leaders of such organizations become beacons of hope, transmitting positive energy to the organization. Therein lies the third lesson in regrouping when things go bad: *leaders must radiate positive energy throughout the organization when things are going well, and especially when they are not.*

When things go bad, the reservoir of resolve in an organization will be drained dry if the leadership is not prepared to replenish the supply. It starts with positive energy—a source of hope and a commitment to create a new future. We all may have worked for someone whose energy gradient was just the opposite of what it was supposed to be. Instead of positive energy, it was toxic energy.

For example, I once worked for an individual who was fond of meetings. Each morning, he demanded you report to his office, where he would sometimes spend hours hashing and rehashing old news. It got to

150

the point where I dreaded these meetings because I could physically feel the energy leaving my body. Others felt the same way—you could see it in their posture as they left the energy drainer's office.

Leaders should never deplete their team members' energy; they should create it. In light of the issues each faced during his terms, can there be any doubt Ford and Lincoln were energy suppliers, not energy drainers?

Culture-driven, people-centered organizations understand the importance of managing the energy supply. Adversity is a fact. Teams deal with adversity all the time. On matters of grave importance, it is crucial for leaders to process the information about the adversity before walking up and down the hall interacting with team members. People must be allowed time to process the information and issues.

From time to time during executive conferences held to discuss difficult issues, I remind our leaders that our coworkers are perceptive. They know we are meeting, and they are waiting patiently to see our facial expressions and our body language as we each leave the room. News travels quickly, which leads to the fourth and final lesson regarding regrouping when things go bad: *find a private place where the team can think clearly and freely.*

Back in the early 1990s, we hired a leadership consulting group, Senn-Delaney, to help our company improve its organizational and individual effectiveness. On the first day of meetings, our management team reluctantly left the work at hand and hurried to an off-site conference center.

The facilitator was a seasoned professional who knew the truth about executives. We were there in body, but we were all thinking about matters at the office. He began by asking the group four questions.

> Have you ever been with someone who was not there?
> Have you ever been with someone and you were not there?
> Have you ever been at a meeting and no one was there?
> Have you ever gone home and left your brain at work?

We could all answer at least one of the questions in the affirmative, but the questions proved the perfect segue for the facilitator to introduce us to a concept Senn-Delaney called, "Be Here Now." The importance of living in the present moment is not new, but distilling the concept into three short words was powerful for us all.

When things go bad (and they will), leaders need a place where they can talk, listen, and remove themselves from the day-to-day chatter of work. The "Be Here Now" concept is made possible only by effort—it is not a natural behavior, especially in this age of cellular telephones, pagers, and personal digital assistants.

At United, we created a "war room" specifically for dealing with important issues. It is isolated, yet it is well equipped with the necessary resources to ensure accurate data from around the organization. The specially made hexagon-shaped table in the room allows all the participants to see one another. The group dynamic of not having a so-called "power position" at the end of a table is astounding. We use the room regularly, and it routinely produces great decisions.

In culture-driven, people-centered organizations, human beings communicate with human beings. Progress is cultivated through a common understanding that solutions are ongoing dialogues for transforming relationships. Even when problems exist, the best course of action is to communicate those issues openly and honestly.

Ford said it best during a commemorative ceremony in 2005 recognizing the thirtieth anniversary of the signing of the Helsinki Final Act. "We were guided by the most basic of principles," he said, "working together toward the peaceful settlement of conflicts, respecting the freedom of thought, conscience, religion and belief, and supporting the self-determination of all to promote a true and lasting peace."

What a powerful image of these leaders from 35 nations communicating with one another at a time when the threat of nuclear annihilation loomed with every conversation between the East and the West. Despite the enormous pressures applied by stakeholders in their own countries, all 35 leaders signed the document. Thirty years later, an additional 20 leaders had signed. What had started as a meeting of leaders in Finland to tackle a vital challenge ultimately turned out to be nothing short of remarkable—an opportunity to change the world for the better.

Being connected to a higher purpose restores hope when things go bad. In 1993, I was stationed in England at RAF Alconbury flying U-2 high-altitude reconnaissance missions. On one particular flight, I encountered a landing gear malfunction that required landing with an inoperable tailwheel, which in the U-2 is used to control the airplane on the ground.

During the landing, the airplane began swerving off the runway and into the infield.

Despite my best efforts to control the aircraft, it left the hard surface and moved straight toward a concrete tower used for aircraft operations. Fortunately, it was a wet English day, and the ground was soft and moist. The plane immediately began to sink into the mud, and it came to an abrupt stop, buried nine feet in the ground about four feet from the concrete structure.

A fellow U-2 pilot who had seen the accident helped me from the aircraft. I recalled the uneasy feeling in my stomach when the wing commander came speeding up to the aircraft, having heard the radio transmission from the tower that the U-2 had encountered a mishap and was off the runway.

In the Air Force, pilots are expected to return planes to the hangar from which they taxi or be prepared to answer tough questions regarding what transpired. You were guilty until proven innocent, and you needed to prove that innocence.

Understandably, commanders were particularly interested in seeing the U-2, which was a national asset worth tens of millions of dollars and which had prototype cameras unlike any others in the world, returned without dents or blemishes.

Right after the crash, I was taken to the hospital, where my minor injuries were treated, and I was directed to visit with a psychologist interested in ascertaining my mental state. In addition, I had a chance to speak with several safety officers regarding the chain of events leading to the mishap.

Afterward, I was placed on administrative leave pending the findings of the aircraft accident investigation team. That process took approximately one week, and during that time I was instructed not to come to the squadron or communicate with fellow pilots. As a result, the break gave me plenty of time to reassess my military career and to contemplate the prospect of reimbursing the government given my junior officer's pay grade—a mammoth payment plan that would extend for centuries.

Subsequent investigation revealed a maintenance issue with the landing gear, and I was exonerated and reinstated to my squadron. After my reinstatement, my commanders said they knew all along it could not have been pilot error. Even so, during that time when my future was in limbo, I was reminded that even when things go bad, the important matters, such as faith and family, do not change.

Albert Einstein once wrote, "In the middle of every difficulty lies an opportunity." We do not always see the opportunity at first; sometimes it takes an objective person to help us do so. In any case, opportunities abound because we have choices to make. We can choose the manner in which adversity shapes our lives and our organizations. We have a choice. I believe God did not create us to endure the future; he created us to embrace the future—to live it.

We know others have triumphed despite adversity. Intellectually, we process the knowledge that Henry Ford went broke five times before achieving success, that Beethoven did not allow his deafness to prevent him from composing symphonies, or that actor James Earl Jones overcame a childhood stuttering problem to develop a voice that made him a legendary spokesman.

A few years ago, United had an intellectual property dispute with a company that was using the name Market Street to market a real estate development in which a supermarket served as an anchor. When it first came to our attention, we asked our legal department to send the customary notification to that company. We received in return a lengthy legal document explaining that the company was using the name as part of a real estate development and not as a supermarket concern.

As the months went by, the legal bills mounted, and neither side's legal team was willing to give ground. Finally, our intellectual property attorney called to advise me that we would most likely have to litigate the case, and the cost could exceed $1 million. He tempered that comment by saying United had a good chance of winning.

To try to prevent litigation, I asked for a meeting with my counterpart using the Market Street trade name. We agreed to meet. Our attorney and I made the trip, and when we walked into the room, there was the principal of the company and five attorneys.

I remember asking our counsel if he had any knowledge of these attorneys. He replied, "I know them all, and they're all expensive."

The attorney and I recognized the meeting was going to be unproductive and expensive. I asked our attorney if it would be permissible to ask their principal to go for a walk around the building, and he told me it would. I asked the opposing team's CEO if he would like to take a walk. Immediately, all five attorneys strenuously objected to our stroll without legal counsel present.

Fortunately, their CEO agreed that a walk might be helpful. The walk turned into lunch and an opportunity to resolve our differences before we returned to a roomful of attorneys to report our successful compromise. The agreement resulted in a business partnership between us. When things go wrong, the best course of action is to get eye to eye with the opposition's leader and seek an equitable solution.

These examples, along with many others, remind us the human spirit is an extraordinarily powerful resource. Culture-driven organizations constantly cultivate this spirit in everyone. Yes, things will go bad from time to time, but regrouping leaves us stronger than before and gives us hope for tomorrow. Consider these words penned by an anonymous poet:

Looking back, it seems to me
All the grief, which had to be,
Left me when the pain was o'er
Richer than I'd been before.

FROM THE EXPRESS LANE

※ Things will go bad—adversity is a fact of life.

※ Make decisions based on principles, not popularity.

※ Make decisions based on a godly perspective, not a worldly perspective.

※ Leaders must create positive energy in an organization, not toxic energy.

※ Create a place of privacy where the team can think clearly and freely

※ With adversity comes opportunities, but they must be sought actively.

※ Healing starts where pride stops.

PART THREE

INTANGIBLES
DRIVE
TANGIBLES

PEOPLE, NOT PROFITS

Stories are important to organizations because they create a sense of community and, in the best of cases, spark a common purpose. In many respects, I like to think of United in this way because our organization is a large body with a common devotion. One of my favorite stories that makes me feel the way I do about United's commitment to its vision involved Keith Bradley, a seasoned store director at the time.

As the story goes, a guest arrived at Keith's store late one afternoon with a serious complaint: in the guest's opinion, we had sold a ham that was out of date and inedible. The guest was visibly upset, and she raised her voice, demanding immediate assistance. "I have out-of-town guests at home waiting to eat, and this ham is no good," she complained. Keith apologized and glanced down at the out-of-date ham, and he discovered something interesting.

The ham the guest had in her hands did not come from United—it was a product sold by a competitor down the street. "Ma'am, we don't sell this brand of ham at United," Keith explained as he pointed to the competitor's logo on the packaging, "but I know you're upset, and so let's go back to the back and find a ham that you'll like, and we'll get you back home right away—no charge."

164

The woman appeared mortified. "I apologize," she said as she walked with Keith to the meat market, "I was running late preparing the dinner, and I asked my husband to pick the ham up on his way home from work. I had no idea he went some place other than United." The woman picked out a ham to serve her guests and happily hurried home, embarrassed by the misunderstanding.

THE STORY IS NOT about a bad ham. Certainly, we have made our share of mistakes during the past 90 years. This is about a store director focusing more on the person than on the profits. We gave away a ham, but we earned her business for life. More important, the woman became a champion for United—an extension of our marketing department—telling the story to anyone who would listen.

At United, we do not have a training manual or policy that reads, "If someone arrives at the store with a bad ham from a competitor, replace it for free." Keith made a great decision because he understood the organization's vision, mission, and commitment to sustainability. In other words, today we would say Keith understood our vision to serve others, our commitment to ultimate service, and our desire to invest something now in exchange for a long-lasting relationship with a guest.

It is worth noting that Keith Bradley never told this story—his fellow team members did. In fact, he said he only vaguely remembers it, and he shrugs the incident off as something any of United's store directors would do in the normal course of duty. I tend to believe him, but it represents a model for our organization to follow—a behavior worthy of emulation because it shows what happens when team members live the organization's vision and mission.

In this example, focusing foremost on people, not on profits, actually proved very profitable over the long haul. More important, the story highlights what happens when a culture-driven, people-centered organization lets go and allows its people to make decisions using their best judgment.

Recently, United embraced a divisional restructuring to capitalize on the individual differences within the chain of stores. Whereas before we operated the nearly 50-store chain in a somewhat homogenized manner, today we manage the chain using three divisions: specialty, international, and traditional. This restructuring allows United to focus on maximizing the potential of each store. The process begins with the type of leader required to direct each store.

For example, large stores typically have more than 450 team members, whereas small stores typically have fewer than 150. In a large store, the store director is a generalist out of necessity and must devote more time to managing relationships and team building. In a small store, the store director often is himself involved in production and must devote more time to specific tasks. By approaching the business with this level of focus, our performance standards have increased exponentially in all our divisions.

Personal experiences and relationships shape thinking. Without question, my sense of the importance of people stems from three vivid memories. I am grateful to have two of them behind me. The third is one I reflect on daily. It was inspiring.

The initial experience occurred during the first Gulf War. During the early morning hours of August 2, 1990, Iraq invaded Kuwait with more than 100,000 soldiers and 700 tanks. At the time, I was a U-2 reconnaissance pilot. Although my wife and I were within 90 days of the arrival of our second child, I was deployed to join other U-2 pilots in a provisional reconnaissance squadron based in Saudi Arabia.

The U-2 Dragon Lady is an aviation marvel. It is built for solo flights at altitudes above 70,000 feet. The pilot wears a pressure suit, similar to those worn by early astronauts. The missions are long, often in excess of nine hours; however, they are meaningful and are worth the physical and mental challenges for the pilot. The pilots assigned to the U-2 program are exceptionally good at what they do. It was an enormous privilege to fly and work with them.

The initial flights over Kuwait showed a massive buildup along the tri-country borders of Iraq, Kuwait, and Saudi Arabia. Using data from the highly sophisticated camera systems installed on the U-2, the White House and military planners got a clear picture of the death and destruction inflicted on the people of

Kuwait. Iraqi jets had bombed targets in the capital city, and enemy Special Forces had landed at the defense ministry and at the Emir's palace. Roadblocks were in place; looting was already well under way. Atrocious behavior was the order of the day in this tiny country under siege.

For more than four months, we flew round-the-clock reconnaissance. The situation continued to deteriorate, and no amount of diplomacy seemed to matter. In early January 1991, Congress gave President George H. W. Bush the authority to wage war. By late January, the air war against Iraq was in full swing, and by February, the ground war had the Iraqi invaders withdrawing toward Baghdad. The road to Basra, littered with death and destruction, was a sad commentary on the value of life.

I was flying a mission over Basra in February 1991. A raging tank battle between soldiers of the 24th Infantry (Mechanized) Division and the Iraqi Republican National Guard caught my attention. Peering through my drift sight, a periscope-like feature in the U-2, I could detail one blast after another. The battle went on for hours.

The command authority directed me to remain overhead and provide imagery to the battlefield commanders below. Eventually, military target planners organized air support, which ultimately allowed the soldiers of the 24th to prevail. At the conclusion of the battle, more than 500 vehicles and 23 T-72 tanks had been destroyed, but, more important, lives were forever changed, including mine. The experience left me with two permanent imprints.

First, contrary to the glamorized war movies I grew up watching, the real experience is a horrible thing. People who claim a desire to see action in war have never seen action in war or they would not make such a statement. Second, people matter. The value of life is exceedingly high. The soldiers killed that day were fellow human beings—regardless of their allegiance.

The second experience occurred while I was serving as a weather reconnaissance pilot in the South Pacific. One aspect of the work I enjoyed a great deal was airdropping supplies to the islanders living on the remote islands of Micronesia. Each year, we would collect supplies—clothing, tools, and fishing gear—and drop them by flying low over the beaches and pushing out boxes tied to parachutes.

From time to time, when we were not flying, we would take fishing boats to visit the islanders, capitalizing on their knowledge of the best reefs for scuba diving. Over time, we established great friendships, and we came to realize that despite their different lifestyles, they were not unlike us—they had families, homes, and responsibilities just as we did.

In August 1984, I was part of a weather reconnaissance team conducting surveillance of Typhoon Ike (like hurricanes, typhoons are tropical cyclones, but they occur in the western Pacific or Indian oceans). Typhoon Ike was a category 4 typhoon with winds of 145 miles per hour. Flying into the eye of a treacherous storm is unlike any other experience. Pilots begin by flying at 1,000 feet above the ocean.

170

On board the aircraft is a weather officer trained in meteorological studies. At 1,000 feet above the ocean, the weather officer can assess the direction and intensity of the waves. If the weather officer cannot see the waves at 1,000 feet because of cloud cover, the pilots fly the aircraft to just 500 feet above the water. This procedure is necessary because it is the most accurate method for determining the storm's actual movement.

The closer the aircraft gets to the storm, the more agitated the water appears. With sustained winds of 100 miles per hour, the ocean looks like a white sheet of churning water—similar to what you might see on the surface of a Jacuzzi. At 100 miles per hour of surface wind, regulations require pilots to climb to 10,000 feet above the ocean to maximize safety during the most dangerous aspect of the mission: penetrating the tight band of thunderstorms known as the eyewall.

With everything onboard strapped down tightly and with shoulder harnesses locked across each crewmember's chest, both pilots actually fly the aircraft into the eye of the storm. Sometimes the dashboard shakes so badly it is difficult to read the gauges. One pilot flies the yoke; the other pilot flies the power. Often, heavy rain makes the radar useless, and it is difficult to navigate around the heaviest thunderstorms.

Because the storm is circulating around a low center of pressure, flying into the eye is like riding a roller coaster during the downward dip. Flying out of the storm is just the opposite. In other words, when you are flying into the storm, the power is almost at idle as you battle for control against the fiercely shifting wind currents, but when you are flying out of the storm, the power is at a maximum—like trying to fly out of a huge imaginary hole.

On this particular mission, the crew witnessed the power of Mother Nature as massive waves swallowed many of the small fishing villages occupied by our Micronesian friends, leaving a path of destruction that

171

is still hard for me to visualize in my mind's eye to this day. Typhoon Ike slammed into the Philippines, killing thousands and leaving nearly 500,000 people homeless.

This second experience, like the first, left me with two permanent imprints. First, the power of nature is beyond comprehension. Typhoon Ike, like Hurricane Katrina, gave me a greater understanding of natural disasters and the indiscriminate horror left in their wake. Second, people matter; the value of life is exceedingly high. The villagers killed during Typhoon Ike were fellow human beings, regardless of their lifestyles.

172

The third experience occurred during a brief assignment as a presidential advance agent working with the White House Travel Office. Rated military pilots are recruited and assigned as liaison officers, responsible for coordinating between the flight crew of Air Force One and civilian airport personnel located in cities scheduled for a presidential stop. The gist of the job is to ensure that the airport is safe, primarily from a pilot's point of view—Secret Service agents handle other security matters associated with the airfield.

Boarding Air Force One is a heady experience. No other airplane in the world exudes power like the one the president uses to travel from place to place. The two custom-built Boeing 747s are flown and maintained by exceptionally dedicated and talented people. All of that aside, my experience went well beyond playing a small role in the safe arrival and departure of the president.

Of greater value to me was observing the humanness of President George H. W. Bush.

During his inaugural speech in 1989, Bush said:

I have spoken of a Thousand Points of Light, of all the community organizations that are spread like stars throughout the Nation, doing good. We will work hand in hand, encouraging, sometimes leading, sometimes being led, rewarding. We will work on this in the White House, in the Cabinet agencies. I will go to the people and the programs that are the brighter points of light, and I'll ask every member of my government to become involved. The old ideas are new again because they're not old; they are timeless: duty, sacrifice, commitment, and a patriotism that finds its expression in taking part and pitching in.

True to his word, Bush, whenever possible, took advantage of his travels across the country to thank citizens for what they were doing in their community. What made these ordinary people interesting was the nature of their accomplishments, which might involve volunteering at a library or building a small park for disabled children. Rather than spending all of his time with wealthy contributors, Bush seemed consumed with ordinary people—people who did not make the headlines.

Following the arrival of Air Force One, Bush would deplane and walk to the people selected for recognition. Normally, the number would be small, fewer than ten or so. Standing next to the massive 747 was a thrill for all of these people, but getting to meet the president was a life-changing experience. During the trips I made with Bush, I witnessed something impressive about him.

As he approached the lineup of accomplished, albeit ordinary, people, Bush called them each by name and thanked them for what they had done in the community. He spoke in surprising detail, often citing specific facts about each person's accomplishments, which, understandably, left everyone mesmerized. It was a thrill to see the president of the United States of America taking a moment to say, "Thank you."

The third experience, like the first two, left me with a couple of permanent imprints. First, the most powerful human being in the free world is still a human being. Bush once said, "A president is neither prince nor pope, and I don't seek a window on men's souls. In fact, I yearn for a greater tolerance, an easygoingness about each other's attitudes and way of life."

More important, Bush saw power as being useful only to the extent that it could help people. "We are given power not to advance our own purposes," he said, "nor to make a great show in the world, nor a name. There is but one just use of power, and it is to serve people." What a splendid statement for a leader—especially a leader seeking to create a sustainable, culture-driven, people-centered organization.

175

An additional imprint of my experience is a familiar one: people matter; the value of life is exceedingly high. *The world we live in today often fails to recognize the value of human beings.* It should not take a war or a natural disaster to remind us of the sanctity of life.

In the supermarket business, we operate in a world of inclusiveness, not exclusiveness. Everyone needs food to survive, and each day, when we open our doors, people from all walks of life arrive. Regardless of their pedigree, they are all fellow human beings worthy of being treated like guests in our homes.

The knowledge-based revolution we live in today promotes the use of data to grow sales, improve profit per customer, and even identify unprofitable accounts that need to be resigned. However, in our zeal to maximize performance, we often forget people really do matter.

Occasionally, when I am asked about "cherry pickers," people who shop our stores only to buy ad items discounted for the week, I reflect on the mental imprints of my past and the higher purpose we seek. My experiences shape my thinking. It may cost us some profit to meet the needs of those guests, but we are still fulfilling our vision of serving and enriching the lives of others, which makes the investment worthwhile.

Focusing foremost on people, not profits, helps organizations realize the unique qualities of human beings—the authenticity found in every life. In the case of United, it has helped our team members recognize the need for outreach. Several years ago, Matt Bumstead, a great-grandson of our founder and a company co-president, created UCrew, an all-volunteer service program where team members get involved in their communities, give back to their neighbors, and strengthen coworker relationships.

Each store's team members conduct approximately six group service activities each year. These activities can be in support of any local charity or church-affiliated organization. UCrew teams have been called upon to carry out such activities as helping to build houses, feeding the needy, working at charitable fundraising events, cleaning up neighborhoods and highways, and assisting local schools.

Development of the UCrew program helped United become the first recipient of the 2003 Community Service Award from *Supermarket News*, the industry's leading trade publication. I mention the award not to heap praise on the program, but to remind culture-driven, people-centered leaders to create opportunities for team members to make an impact on their communities.

We know, of course, that when profits soar and times are good, many leaders make financial commitments to people-centered programs that promote community outreach, among other things. But what happens when times are lean? Too often, when organizations fail to realize their profit projections, people-centered programs quickly disappear—they are seen by leaders as an unnecessary expense.

Our modern-day culture suggests that leaders should be focused exclusively on what team members bring to the job, ignoring other factors occurring off the job that might affect their performance. A culture-driven, people-centered leader recognizes that integrity requires a more integrated way of thinking that considers all aspects of a team member's life, both on the job and off the job.

An example of this at United involved a team member with more than 30 years of service who had recently been diagnosed with cancer. There was no doubt this diagnosis would have an impact on his job, and to pretend it would not or that we should not be concerned about his personal well-being was to deny reality.

178

Rather than skirt the issue, we opted to work with the team member in a proactive manner that would benefit his family and allow him to continue to fill a productive role in our organization. Sadly, this particular team member died, but had we followed the conventional advice on such matters, we would have allowed the benefits system to run its course, and in doing so we might have undermined the quality of life this team member deserved during his final days.

To maintain this approach, we have limited the number of stores and the number of people one supervisor oversees. We try to limit supervisors to no more than eight direct reports, and we try to limit the number of stores one supervisor oversees to ten or fewer. This runs counter to conventional industry wisdom in multistore enterprises, where it is not uncommon to have one supervisor responsible for anywhere from 30 to 200 stores.

When you have a manageable number of stores or team members to oversee, you can assure yourself of making an impact—and making a difference.

Making a difference requires more time and energy because different people have different experiences and different needs despite serving in the same work environment. *People are always more important than the process.*

Because they see human beings as assets, not expenses, culture-driven, people-centered organizations are different. They remain steadfast in their commitment, focusing foremost on people, not profits. In return, their people find ways to generate the necessary profits to ensure the organization's sustainability. These are the organizations deserving of a legacy worth remembering. This is the spirit worth cultivating because it embraces the truth: intangibles drive tangibles.

FROM THE EXPRESS LANE

※ Empower people to make decisions based on the organization's vision, mission, and commitment to sustainability.

※ Focusing on people instead of profits will prove profitable in the long term.

※ Regardless of who they are or where they live, people matter. The value of life is exceedingly high.

※ Ordinary people are capable of extraordinary deeds.

※ Focusing on the authenticity of people requires re-alizing their unique qualities and contributions as human beings.

AISLE **10**

DECISION MAKING: MORE THAN A SPREADSHEET

We learn from our mistakes. In the mid-1990s, we opened a store in Amarillo, Texas. At the time, the store offered the best and most customer-friendly technology in the supermarket industry. The bakery department was an area of particular focus for our company. We had high expectations, and we thought the department would serve as a difference maker in terms of freshness and quality—important considerations for all guests visiting the store.

Like most retailers, we based our decision to build the store largely on data supplied by real estate sources detailing growth trends, the potential available dollars in the trade area, the per-capita weekly expenditure for food, and the simple attraction the store represented. In those days, we had an undeveloped marketing department.

In fact, we had three full-time team members and one or two part-time interns working their way through college. The staff dedicated virtually all of its time to advertising, not marketing. As a result, new-store construction was a team decision based on spreadsheets and corresponding data. In the case of our new Amarillo store, the numbers justified the opening.

Each week following the grand opening, our leaders would study the financial reports on the store's performance. Interestingly, despite great numbers from the store in general, we noticed the bakery department was underperforming. We were not realizing the numbers we had projected. Sitting in our offices 120 miles away and studying the spreadsheets, it appeared we had missed something. Leaders began quizzing the bakery director, who, in turn, began quizzing the bakery manager at the store, seeking answers for the lackluster performance. Initially, the thought surfaced that we might have quality issues, but the recipes were the same as those used in our other stores, and the bakery team had not made changes.

Our attention soon focused on the people in the bakery. Wrongly, we assumed we had to make a change in leadership at the bakery manager position. Sales remained flat. Frustrated and confused by the bakery's performance, we formed a small team to thoroughly investigate the problem.

We left our offices, made the two-hour drive up the interstate, checked into hotel rooms, and camped at the store for a week. We asked questions of guests and observed the daily traffic. Three days after immersing ourselves in the store, we realized our problem: a large percentage of the guests shopping the store were empty nesters. We had neither a quality issue nor a leadership issue. We had a packaging issue.

Empty nesters were not interested in buying a dozen doughnuts, nor were they motivated to purchase anything by the dozen. They wanted smaller portion sizes. We validated our findings by observing similar trends in the meat market, where large packages of ground meat were not selling, either.

Hurriedly, we changed our packaging. Eureka! Sales for doughnuts, bagels, and other bakery *products increased, and the store's performance improved.*

S INCE I WAS SERVING as marketing director at the time, I felt bad about what had happened. As a result, I pledged to improve my decision-making process. Working with my team, we created a new decision-making model, one that would have prevented the bakery fiasco in our Amarillo store.

The model shown here consists of three buckets of information. One contains information directly from guests, the buyers of our products and services. A second bucket contains information from the sellers—the collective intuition and knowledge of seasoned professionals. The third bucket contains empirical information, data based on actual performance.

Buyer's Intuition

Seller's Intuition

Empirical Data

Business decisions are challenging enough when leaders possess data from all three buckets, but a decision made using data from only one bucket, regardless of which bucket it is, is problematic. *If decision makers hope to bring about satisfactory resolution, they need a balanced protocol.* The three-bucket approach to decision making for organizational leaders is similar to the triangulation method of navigation used by pilots, sailors, and explorers.

Feedback from each bucket allows an organizational leader to move one step closer to confidently establishing a bearing, a position. One data source can provide a faulty signal, but having a second source and, better yet, a third source exponentially narrows the margin for error.

185

In the case of the first bucket of data, buyers' intuition is valuable, but only in the context of human emotion. Suppose a supermarket chain initiated a program at store level to stock every single item asked for during the course of a day, a month, or a year. Even with a virtual inventory capability utilizing online suppliers, the space required to manage the physical store inventory would be staggering, and the amount of perishable product discarded because of a lack of sales would make the cost of this initiative prohibitive.

The truth is, buyers can put an organization out of business without even thinking twice about it. A guest who wants one special jar of dressing for a meal she is preparing has little regard for the fact that dressings are sold to the retailer not by the individual unit, but by the case. She is more than willing to buy one jar, but the rest of the case is someone else's problem. The buyer's feedback is suspect only because it is born out of emotion rather than reason. The decision to buy or not to buy is one of "feeling"—a decision made from the heart, not from the head. The heart contains telling information, but it is prone to exaggerate the truth and view the world from a myopic perspective.

The second bucket of information contains its pitfalls, as well. A seller's intuition offers immediate insight, but it too represents a "feeling" decision. Little reasoning goes into formulating a seller's intuition. Instead, sellers rely on emotional mental imprints rather than on objective reasoning.

For example, supermarkets have a wide variety of selling programs running concurrently. In addition to their own product offerings, supermarkets will allow business partners to stock and sell books, newspapers, magazines, and greeting cards, among other things. A profit-sharing arrangement allows such programs to be mutually beneficial. Full-service programs, where the supply partner ensures adequate stock by having its people service the stores, free up the store's team members for other tasks.

When shelf space in a store is tight, some store directors may suggest reducing or eliminating such programs. Their intuition tells them they do not sell much of the product because the rack is always full. In other words, products in the store that require handling by the store director and staff are either restocked, which means they are selling, or dusted, which means they are not selling. Good operators have a mental imprint of what sells and what does not.

187

These tangible signs of success or failure provide operators with an impression of the movement of one product relative to another; however, with full-service programs, the racks appear to be full all the time by design, and therefore, some store directors may not fully appreciate the movement of the product because they are not restocking the item daily. Their intuition tells them the product is a failure. In short, they are susceptible to being fooled into feeling that a product is not selling when it may be selling just fine.

Like a pilot attempting to fly in bad weather without instruments to provide objective information, relying exclusively on feeling is fraught with danger. Without other means of calibration, pilots flying in bad weather using the "seat-of-the-pants" method typically crash. Likewise, decision makers who rely exclusively on intuition as the basis for making a decision will most likely crash, too.

The third bucket contains empirical information—good, solid, factual data—but even empirical data can steer a decision maker wrong. If we were in church, some might say these next few sentences represent "hard teaching." Organizations absolutely love numbers. Some people just cannot seem to get enough numbers. In the mid-1990s, it became fashionable to offer a frequent shopper card or a loyalty card, where customers received discounts and other benefits in exchange for supplying their personal data to a retailer.

The theory was simple. The retailer would track each customer's personal buying habits and then tailor messaging and sales offers to that customer in a specific manner. The retailer would learn who its best customers were, and, in exchange, the customers would receive information from the retailer specifically targeted to them. Coke drinkers would not receive ads for Pepsi or vice versa, and so on. It seemed like a logical initiative.

What no one really took into consideration at the time was the sheer amount of information contained in just one store's transactional file for just one day. In many supermarkets, it was enough green-bar computer paper to fill an entire conference room from floor to ceiling. The fact is, organizations are inundated with numbers, which brings us to another weakness of data: without accurate processing of the data, proper use of the resulting information is impossible.

Is it possible that inaccurate accounting could be a problem in this high-tech age? Regrettably, the answer is a resounding yes, and the errors are material. Home Depot, for example, announced at the end of 2006 that its incorrect accounting for stock options during the previous 26 years resulted in almost $200 million of unrecorded expense. There are a number of similar examples.

The enormous challenge of deciphering financial accounting standards these days can make empirical data seem more theoretical than necessary, even when the best intentions are clear. Accounting is just a fuzzy business. I recall an accounting professor remarking that accounting is more art than science. He would typically draw a laugh from class members because his initial response to virtually any accounting question was, "It depends." Despite the humor, his response was truthful. *The fact is, spreadsheets and their corresponding numbers, while useful, are often insufficient for sound decision making.*

It is balance that is needed. The three-bucket decision-making model is a quick tool to give leaders who are charged with making decisions the discipline to explore the facts before rendering a judgment. One variable that often complicates matters is the issue of time—more specifically, a lack of time. It is a real issue with real ramifications.

Many of America's best business schools utilize a time-bound teaching game called "Looking Glass" to help leaders gain a better understanding of decision making. The game's details are confidential, but participants are randomly assigned leadership roles inside fictitious companies. Each team is graded on the number of issues it deals with of more than 50 that necessitate certain decisions within a finite amount of time. At the end of the game, the team that has identified the most issues and made the most "good" decisions wins.

Participants generally end the game with a greater appreciation for two things. First, stress (brought about by the time constraints in the game) has an adverse effect on meaningful communication. Second, the farther removed a senior leader is from the front-line members of the team, the less knowledge that person has of the issues.

Most teams fail to identify even half of the relevant issues, and, of those issues identified, senior leaders are apprised of only a small percentage. What makes the game a compelling teaching tool is participants on each team receive the data necessary to identify the issues before the game begins. Their failure to successfully navigate the game and make the appropriate decisions is a function of time and poor communication.

For example, I was fascinated at the end of the game to see what percentage of the issues actually made it from midlevel management to top management. The year I played, our team took first place in spite of the fact that we identified only 65 percent of the issues. Of those we identified, only 27 percent were communicated to the CEO of the business.

The lesson for decision makers is threefold. First, decision makers need more than one source of data before making a judgment. In considering which buckets of data to rely upon, empirical data should be first on the list only because they are the only source that is not affected by emotion. *Striking a balance between subjective data and objective data is important to good decision makers.*

Second, decision makers must recognize time constraints create stress, which hinders communication between individuals with knowledge and individuals with decision-making authority. Forethought and planning can mitigate many of the crisis-type decisions necessary in a pinch.

For example, contingency plans, disaster-preparedness exercises, and continuity documentation can alleviate much of the stress caused by a shortage of time. In reality, most situations do not require an immediate decision, although as leaders we like to convince ourselves that we must hurriedly react to situations. A little patience can pay big dividends.

Finally, decision makers must acknowledge that the further removed they are from the front-line members of the team, the more selective the information they receive becomes. The knowledge of what is working and what is not working resides with the people charged with executing on a daily basis. Getting face to face with them and the people they interact with— the buyers of their products and services—ensures an information flow that almost certainly would not otherwise occur.

This truism is more a reflection of poor listening skills than an unfavorable observation regarding leaders and their willingness to share information. When we seriously employ our listening skills, we gain a better understanding of people, which, in turn, improves our ability to make good decisions.

Shortly after I became United's CEO in 2004, our team instituted a "flash call," a weekly conference call between the senior field supervisors and the store support center's administrators. The call takes place at 7:30 a.m. sharp each Tuesday. What is good about the call is all senior leaders sit and listen. They do very little talking. As a result, we learn all sorts of things.

We also have the opportunity to hear the inflections in the voices of those at the tip of the sword—those wonderful, indispensable folks who interact with guests. In the same way the famous Wal-Mart Saturday morning meeting helped shrink the massive discounter and allow it to stay connected, the "flash call" changed us. Before we started with the conference call, we might get an e-mail that electrical power in a store went down for 30 minutes or that a register failed three times that week, but we would go about our daily business without really appreciating the magnitude of such problems.

The issues seemed minor from our perspective; however, from the perspective of a store director or a team member ringing up groceries, the issues were understandably major. Having a system down or a register out for 30 minutes on a Friday afternoon is unacceptable, especially if you happen to be standing in the checkout lane at the wrong time.

After we started the conference call, there was no escaping the truth; everyone in the room heard the pain and frustration in the field supervisor's voice first-hand. The weekly call provided a commodity senior leaders in large organizations rarely get: direct feedback from the troops in the field. We could feel their pain and their elation.

For example, during a recent ice storm, the flash call was invaluable to senior leaders seeking information on which stores were short on inventory. Circumstances were changing so rapidly that it affected our standard method of communication.

Now that we have been using the flash call program for years, our leaders exhibit a different sense of urgency from what they used to demonstrate. We have learned to listen more effectively. Consequently, our decision making has improved, as well. We are far from perfect, and relevant information

194

occasionally fails to make it to us, but we are steadily improving.

Decision making requires much more than a spreadsheet. It is a challenging aspect of leadership that mandates a balanced approach—a protocol for assessing the next steps. A culture-driven, people-centered organization creates an environment that requires leaders to listen to front-line team members and remove obstacles in a manner that builds trust and open communication.

FROM THE EXPRESS LANE

- ❋ Sometimes the system, not the people, is the problem that needs to be addressed.

- ❋ Leaders need more than one source of data to make any decision.

- ❋ Explore the facts, and take time to know the facts, before rendering a judgment.

- ❋ Patience should be a leaders best friend when a tough decision must be made.

- ❋ Planning and attention to detail will mitigate the impact of stress on communication.

- ❋ There is no substitute for listening to front-line team members.

THE 4P MANAGEMENT SYSTEM

Galen Walters is among the most influential mentors in my life. Walters is the founder and CEO of Houston, Texas–based adplex. It was clear from our first meeting in 1995 that we would work together. We shared a common belief in God, agreed on the most prominent issues facing businesses, and felt a compelling urge to enrich the lives of others.

Hollywood film producers should be scrambling for the rights to Galen Walters' story. A product of a hardscrabble upbringing, Walters found traditional schooling uninteresting. Sitting in class and bored, he occasionally found himself doodling. Over the course of time, he discovered he had a remarkable gift for drawing.

He graduated from high school and enrolled in the Texas Academy of Art while working for Safeway, where he perfected his talent in illustration and advertising design. After graduation, he moved to the advertising department as a layout artist. During the next seven years he worked his way up to advertising supervisor but left Safeway when he was accepted into the Houston Fire Department.

In 1981, Walters started his own company specializing in the design and printing of weekly advertising circulars while still fighting fires. Safeway became his largest client; he printed millions of circulars for it every week. Over time, other supermarket chains moved their business to Walters, and his company rapidly grew into a multimillion-dollar enterprise. Walters became a millionaire, but he never lost his sense of humility. He gave much of the money away to churches and friends in need; for example, he decided at one point to replace the dilapidated air-conditioning units in the sleeping quarters of several Houston fire stations.

By the mid-1990s, Walters was searching for an easier way to manage his business. He read book after book about management, frequently implementing possible solution after possible *solution, but nothing seemed to click. He found every time his leadership team implemented a solution for an issue in one area of the business, other areas suffered.*

Walters knew the importance of human beings. First and foremost, he understood the importance of the people inside the company, his employees. He also valued people outside the company, partners such as suppliers, bankers, and customers. He understood the need for a focus on performance, but he also knew from experience that performance, particularly in a manufacturing facility, was largely a function of an efficient process.

199

In 1995, Walters developed a new way to manage his business; he called it "The 4Ps of Management." The trademarked system required managers to address issues related to people, process, partners, and performance with equal interest.

The system worked and allowed Walters to explore new opportunities for diversifying the business, adding marketing services with a focus on writing software programs, managing content, and automating the ad-building process. Today, in addition to printing circulars for supermarket chains across the country, his company helps manage the digital content of some of America's best-known companies—NASCAR Images, Hewlett-Packard, and American Airlines, among others.

WHEN I JOINED the company in 1997 as president of the imaging companies, the 4Ps were paving the way for growth. Working together, the adplex executive team refined and enhanced the 4Ps to maximize effectiveness. We purchased several companies in a relatively short amount of time, but by approaching each acquisition from the same perspective (with an eye on categorizing every aspect of the operation into the areas of people, process, partners, and performance), the due diligence was easier.

Understanding the 4Ps starts with the observation that management begins and ends with human beings—people and partners. What happens in

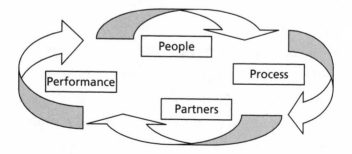

between is a matter of inputs and outputs (process), and what happens afterward is a reflection of results (performance). In other words, the order of the 4Ps makes a difference.

In misaligned cultures, organizations prefer the opposite, beginning with performance and ending with human beings. In a culture-driven, people-centered organization, especially one operating in a knowledge-based area, human beings hold the keys to sustainable success.

Walters taught me a hard but good lesson one day regarding the order of the 4Ps. Whenever our travels permitted, it was common for us to visit our manufacturing plants together. Normally, I had a mental list of everything I wanted to accomplish during the visit, but frequently the list became so long I had to record it on paper. Upon arrival at a plant, I would steadily start ticking off things on my list.

In military-like fashion, I found I could inspect a manufacturing plant in less than one hour. Walters, on the other hand, took half a day. Whereas for me, making a plant visit was a mission, for Walters, making a plant visit was a ministry. As he walked through the facility making mental notes, he took time to visit with individuals along the way.

Finally, one day it came to a head. After visiting one of our plants, we climbed into the car to travel to the airport, and I commented to Galen on how long it took him to make his way through one of the plants. I told him I thought we could accomplish a lot more if he would pick up his pace.

"Dan, you will never be a CEO if you don't recognize the value of the people working in these plants. They see me two or three times each year—they look forward to it, and so do I," he responded.

Then I realized his conversations were sometimes business-related but more often personal. He might visit with one team member about a summer fishing trip to Colorado, or he might talk with another team member about the birth of a child. It did not matter to Walters; he was genuinely interested in simply listening. Since many team members had grown up around Walters, they shared a common bond, a personal respect and admiration for each other.

It was a splendid, albeit hard, leadership lesson for me. I was moving too fast for my own good. Walters was being strategic, and I was being tactical. He was securing relationships, and I was completing checklists. He was right, and I was wrong.

202

The 4Ps concept begins with the people inside the organizations—the team members responsible for carrying out the day-to-day tasks necessary to operate the business.

The next element of the model is process, which is nothing more than a series of inputs and outputs. In a perfect world, a visual depiction of a process looks like two lines running parallel with each other.

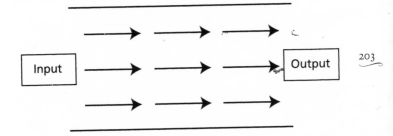

The ideal process contains no bottlenecks or disruptions. The flow is smooth and uninterrupted from beginning to end. This model represents the most efficient process possible; there are no obstructions whatsoever, which results in superior performance. Of course, few processes look like this model. More often than not, the process model looks more like a series of pinch points.

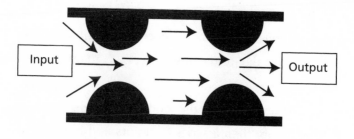

Everything that happens inside an organization is a process. The key to improving performance is the elimination of as many obstructions in the process as possible. The further removed leaders are from the actual process, the harder it is for them to determine what is causing the obstruction. The sources of that information are the teams that use the process every day. They know precisely where the obstructions are located because they must work around those obstructions to carry out their duties.

Recently, our team started mapping the process of constructing departments within new stores. Rather than drawing a box and then dictating to the users the exact amount of space allotted, we actively solicited input from the teams working in each department. We provided sales survey analysis showing the projected volume for the store and for their department. We then asked the team members already working in similar departments in other stores what they would change about their setup.

Not surprisingly, the information was valuable. Some teams suggested more space, and others recommended rearranging the location of certain equipment. Our design team assembled mock-ups of the departmental layout in a large warehouse where team members could see firsthand what we were planning to construct. By seeking input from the users, the designers saved thousands of dollars in change orders once construction began.

More important, the department's efficiency improved because the day-to-day users had input into ways to eliminate the obstructions and streamline the process. Had we simply constructed the stores without assembling the mock-ups and soliciting the users' feedback, the obstructions to the processes would have gone unnoticed initially.

Culture-driven, people-centered organizations understand human beings directly influence process and subsequent performance. *Great ideas can spring from anyone in an organization. The culture of the organization dictates whether they surface.* Even the newest recruits provide organizations with something unique: no blind spots. Human beings are prone to develop a scotoma once they have been in the same environment for a long period. Newcomers see things for what they are, unhindered by the blind spots that develop over time. Organizations ought to seek every newcomer's opinion regarding the workplace within 90 days of that person's reporting for work.

Several years ago, our organization got serious about eliminating inefficiencies. We encouraged every team member to share ideas and recommendations for running a better company. We received remarkable feedback. One team member working in accounting offered this observation: "I work late sometimes, and when I leave the building, I notice a lot of the lights in the offices are left on. It seems like a waste of money."

She was right. We learned the cleaning crew had a system every night of turning on the lights in all the offices as a means of identifying which ones had been cleaned. If a light was off at the end of the cleaning, it meant the crew had missed an office. Our facilities team met with the cleaning crew to develop a more efficient process, which resulted in an annual savings of thousands of dollars.

One of our administrative team members made a similar observation. "I noticed that the window cleaners come too often—half the time they're cleaning clean windows." She was right as well. By changing to a more efficient process, the organization again realized an annual savings of several thousand dollars. Over time, the recommendations of our team members throughout the organization led to millions of dollars in annual savings.

Culture is everything in an organization. One particularly effective leader I followed early in my career had a three "but, sir" rule. Regardless of the topic or the time, everyone in the organization understood it was permissible to share a contrary view. After the third "but sir," if the leader did not agree with your viewpoint, he would say, "I understand your position, and I appreciate your input, but this is what we're going to do."

Sometimes, the leader, after hearing an opinion contrary to his own, would change his mind. In any case, the culture of the organization was one in which followers knew they had a voice, and they had the freedom to express their opinions. The procedure was civil and conversational rather than angry and contentious, which meant the principles of respect and dignity formed the foundation of the process.

Thinking in terms of processes helps team members grasp big challenges without being overwhelmed. All complex operations are composed of small processes. When we properly alter a process, we are literally altering the outcome, creating a better future and hope for the organization.

For as far back as I can remember, my family has cheered for the Dallas Cowboys. The Cowboys enjoyed great success in the 1970s, especially during the era of quarterback Roger Staubach. During those glory years, Tom Landry, the legendary coach of the Cowboys, hired Howard "Red" Hickey to help with the team. Hickey's official titles included coach's assistant and player scout, but his real purpose for being in Dallas was teaching the shotgun offense to Staubach.

208

Landry knew Staubach's running ability would be less effective as he got older, but protecting the team's valuable star player and the organization's prize investment was of greater concern. Landry recruited Hickey, the man most responsible for "inventing" the shotgun offense while an assistant coach with the San Francisco 49ers in the mid-1960s. Hickey changed the process by which Staubach received the football, allowing him more time to execute plays.

As a result, the team's overall performance improved, and the Cowboys went on to win four National Football Conference titles and two Super Bowls. Today, virtually every team in the National

Football League uses the shotgun formation to improve the passing performance of its quarterback.

Amazon.com is another good example of an organization altering a process to enhance performance. The company has used technology to change the process of buying products online, making it easier to serve customers. For example, I enjoy old movies, especially old World War II movies. I also like movies starring Cary Grant, Jimmy Stewart, and John Wayne.

Through the creative use of permissions-granted technology, Amazon.com knows my specific preferences. When old movies about World War II or movies featuring the stars I like become available, I receive a short e-mail making me aware of the offering, usually with an incentive to purchase.

In addition, when the promotional e-mail specifically targeting me arrives, it includes a list of the movies I already own, which prevents me from purchasing the same movie twice. As a result, a relationship of trust has formed between the people at Amazon and me. The relationship is mutually beneficial—I get the movies I want, and they get the performance they seek.

The third element in the 4Ps is partners, a term used to identify the importance of suppliers and buyers—

customers, guests, and users of the products and services sold by an organization. No organization can claim total independence today. It takes suppliers working diligently behind the scenes to ensure success.

In the supermarket industry, for example, except in a few departments such as bakery, floral, and food service, few of the products sold are actually prepared from scratch by team members at the store. Instead, supermarkets rely on a network of thousands of farmers, ranchers, anglers, producers, and brokers, in addition to logistical supply-chain experts, truck drivers, and distribution facilities. Without these partnerships, the experience would be anything but "super."

It seems logical all organizations would place a high value on their partners, given the interdependent nature of these indispensable relationships, but this is often not the case. During the past 50 years, customers or guests have become a necessary inconvenience for many organizations. Rather than embracing and celebrating the people who purchase their products and services, such organizations merely tolerate them. When this happens, few, if any, organizations realize sustained success.

Think about your own experiences along these lines. When was the last time a seller actually made you feel good about the transaction? These days, customers or guests become mesmerized if the salesperson calls them by name. Such is the case with a small mom-and-pop restaurant I frequent—when I get ready to leave, they always say, "Thanks for coming in, Dan." I know it sounds crazy, but I love it when they do that. *Treating customers like partners is often overlooked, but it is important to culture-driven, people-centered organizations.*

Superior performance is a reflection of well-conceived and properly executed processes. Organizations committed to improved performance must seek to remove the obstructions present within the day-to-day tasks. Arbitrary headcount or program reductions may create immediate growth, but sustainable success requires altering the processes—the roots that allow performance to grow.

Culture-driven, people-centered organizations recognize poor performance is symptomatic of deeper problems—problems that require engaging people and changing processes. In this view, performance measurements are mere indicators—tools that prompt additional investigation and productive questioning. Performance measurements alone prompt more questions than they answer.

In addition to the clarity brought about by the 4Ps, performance is enhanced through the use of goals and controls to ensure the team remains focused. Every month, team members from departmental levels through senior management internally publish goals that are vital to the success of their area.

As a result, the company gets traction, and team members realize success as it relates to the annual goals established by the company's shareholders. Mutually agreed-upon goals create a high level of accountability and highlight each team member's professional contribution to the organization's success.

212

Mastering the art of balance in managing an organization requires a heavy focus on issues that matter. The 4Ps are a powerful method for identifying what is important. This method begins and ends with human beings, but between the key categories of people and partners, the importance of process cannot be overstated. When organizations create a culture that promotes human interaction and constantly enhances the processes used in the day-to-day tasks, the result is superior performance.

FROM THE EXPRESS LANE

❈ Management begins and ends with human beings—people and partners.

❈ Culture-driven, people-centered organizations understand human beings directly influence process and subsequent performance.

❈ Culture dictates whether great ideas will spring from anyone in the organization.

❈ Organizations desiring improved performance must seek to remove the obstructions present in the day-to-day processes.

❈ Treating customers and suppliers as partners is important for organizations seeking to enjoy sustained success.

❈ Mutually agreed-upon goals create a higher level of accountability.

HUMILITY
TRUMPS PRIDE

*Several years ago, I met one of the advertising
executives at American Airlines responsible for
managing the company's intellectual property. It was
a huge task, but it could be made much easier with a
computer software solution. As a principal in a small
firm known for designing intellectual property
solutions, I was particularly eager to sit down with
the executive's staff and learn about the difficulty—
the pinch points in the data process. Over the course
of about six months, members of my staff and the
American Airlines staff became friends. Our due
diligence, along with their willingness to share their
ideas, positioned our company as a logical partner.
American Airlines needed a customized solution.*

One day, the American Airlines executive called me with a request. "Dan," he said, "you've spent nearly a half year reviewing our needs. You probably know more about what kind of solution we need than we do. A large advertising agency based in New York City is coming in to make a presentation next week. I'd like you to attend." The request seemed a bit odd given that my company, like the agency, was vying for the business; however, we shared a high level of trust, so I agreed to come as an observer.

The meeting room was large, and about 25 people attended, mostly representatives from the agency making the pitch. After we had all taken our seats, the senior executive from the ad agency began. He was an articulate speaker, and his high-tech presentation was impressively polished. No one else in the room said anything. His portion of the meeting lasted nearly two hours.

I watched my American Airlines friends carefully as they sat and listened. Once the ad agency executive stopped, he said, "This concludes my presentation. I think you can see that it is clearly the right solution for American Airlines. Are there any questions?" Sitting at the opposite end of the long conference table, the American Airlines executive raised his hand.

"What's your question?" asked the ad executive.

"My name is Larry," the decision maker remarked.

"Yes, Larry, what's your question?" the ad executive asked again.

"I don't have a question. I just thought you might like to know my name."

The room became awkwardly quiet. The American Airlines team, including Larry, got up and left the room. The ad agency reps returned to Madison Avenue. Needless to say, the agency did not get American's business.

Some months after the meeting, Larry privately shared his feelings regarding the agency's presentation. "Can you believe the arrogance of the guy making that pitch? He flies down here and whisks his way into a meeting with absolutely no effort to understand our specific issues, no regard for our unique needs, and then he has the audacity to claim that it's 'clearly the right solution for American Airlines,'" he said.

I am not sure what the ad agency executive or his entourage thought went wrong in the meeting—if it even registered that pride fractured the agency's chances of landing the account. My guess is it did not strike a chord with any of the agency people present because they could not see what everyone else in the room could: two hours of self-promotion followed by one hugely arrogant statement. In a way, it was sad because the company had a lot to offer American Airlines. I am certain a great many of the presenter's coworkers had toiled diligently to produce such robust software. He had every reason to be proud of what his company had to offer, but a little humility might have saved his day.

T HE SINGLE BIGGEST THREAT to an organization's success is pride. We are all susceptible to it, and, most likely, we have all fallen victim to it at times. Years ago, a mentor sent me to a management training seminar requiring a 360-degree peer evaluation. Upon arrival, I noticed the room in which we were holding the meeting contained large posters with descriptive words but no names associated.

Shortly after the meeting began, the facilitator asked each participant to find the poster best describing his or her personality. After a brief time, only one poster remained, and it was mine.

The poster read, "Intense, Focused, Driven." I was stunned. I could think of many adjectives to describe my personality, but *intense* would not have been one of them. The facilitator commented that my assessment suggested peers communicate with me using three simple rules: Be brief. Be bright. Be gone. I was embarrassed and humbled. And for the first time in my life, I realized that my own self-perception fell short of my peers' perception of me. In a culture-driven, people-centered organization, honest feedback is a must.

I suppose there is a reason the book of Proverbs listed pride as number one on God's hate list, above lying and the shedding of innocent blood, among others. The Bible records a couple of interesting stories of King David's life in which innocent blood is shed. In the first story, David's adultery with Bathsheba results in four deaths. In the second story, David's prideful census of his army results in 70,000 deaths. I believe the purpose of these stories is to reinforce the destructive nature of pride.

Pride is an interesting word in the English language because it has multiple meanings, some of them in direct conflict with one another. For example, one definition of pride involves a feeling of elation or satisfaction over one's achievements (a positive use of the word), while another suggests a high or overbearing opinion of one's worth or importance.

Culture-driven, people-centered organizations seek to maximize the feeling of elation and satisfaction derived from achievement and minimize any high or overbearing opinion of one's worth or importance. When it comes to pride, maximizing the good and minimizing the bad is a three-step process.

First, organizations must keep people focused on the future, not the past. *The destructive nature of pride is reinforced by what people have done, not what they have yet to do.* Culture-driven, people-centered organizations are always moving toward what they want to become, as opposed to basking in their accomplishments.

At United, for example, the team is always thinking about the company's long-term potential, not its 90 years of history. Jeff Immelt, CEO of General Electric, said, "Most people inside GE learn from the past but have a healthy disrespect for history." Immelt's statement is powerful, considering GE was selected the most admired company in America in 2006 by *Fortune* magazine (the organization has achieved the honor six times in the past decade).

In 2006, magazine editor Geoffrey Colvin coauthored *Secrets of Greatness*. In the book, he wrote of GE, "It's all about the long term. No other U.S. company has been dominant for as long as GE. Of the 12 firms that Charles Dow put into his original Dow Jones industrial average in 1896, GE is the only one still in the index, and most of the others are dead. Survival is another achievement to admire."

A focus on the future keeps people motivated to achieve whatever is necessary for sustained success. At United we say, "A splendid 90-year history does not guarantee another year." If people approach their work with the understanding that survival is another achievement to admire, the prospect of pride's getting a foothold is slim.

Second, *organizations must keep people focused on the pursuit of excellence, not the path to mediocrity.* The pursuit of excellence forces people to confront their weaknesses, adapt their thinking, and keep their egos in check. For example, Tiger Woods is the greatest golfer in the world. How great? In 2003, touring pros selected him Player of the Year, even though he failed to win a major championship or win the most money.

I glanced at an article by David Owen about Woods in a 2006 issue of *Men's Vogue*. Without reading the story, I assumed there was no light left to shed on golf's most celebrated player. I was wrong. Dr. Gio Valiante, a respected psychologist who coaches professional golfers, called my attention to the article and the unique observation Owen made regarding Woods. Owen wrote:

> If there is a graspable key to Woods, it may be this: Everything makes him better. When he was eight, he learned to beat twelve-year-olds by turning his weakness into an edge: He couldn't hit the ball as far as they could, so he taught himself to outthink them. When he got a little older and was long and wild off the tee, he made inaccuracy an advantage, by assembling what has become the most complete recovery game in the history of golf. (As a boy, playing with his father in the evenings, Woods would throw three balls into the trees on each hole, setting himself the challenge of holing all three in cumulative even par or better.) Married players used to complain that bachelorhood gave Woods more time to practice and they were right: Being single was one of his advantages. Now that he's married, though, his edge is being married. . . . Everything makes him better.

Tiger Woods could be a poster child for pride, but he is not. He is a professional on a mission to realize as much of his potential as possible. Organizations should learn from Woods's example. Woods is not a competitor; he is a "surpetitor"—a person striving to *surpass* golfers, not simply play *with* golfers. He is comparing himself not to his peers, but to a different standard—one even he has yet to attain. The result is a remarkable journey characterized by humility despite total dominance over his peers. Like Woods, people inside organizations can embark on the same journey.

Finally, organizations must keep people focused on the right kind of role models. People gain inspiration from leaders who are humble yet effective at asking the right questions—questions that force individuals and teams to reconsider their own biases. The process is one of discovery. My own experience along these lines points to Forrest Whitlow.

Back in 1981, Whitlow was the bookstore manager on the campus of Lubbock Christian College. Meeting nice people was an everyday occurrence on a Christian college campus, but meeting Whitlow was different—he went beyond nice. At the time, I was considering entering military service, and someone had told me that Whitlow was a veteran, so I arranged a time when we could meet.

Whitlow wore a cardigan sweater, Dockers, and Hush Puppies the first time we sat down to talk about the Air Force. Candidly, he looked more like Mister Rogers than like a military man. His office, located in the back of the store, was functional but small. As I sat down, I could see pictures of his children neatly placed on the credenza behind him.

"I understand you used to be in the Air Force," I said.

"Yes, that's right; I retired from the service," he politely responded.

Then something interesting happened. I noticed a small picture of an airplane lying on the desk near his chair. "Were you a pilot in the Air Force?" I asked.

"Yes, I was," he said. "I got to fly most of my career."

Somewhat surprised by the statement, I asked, "What kind of airplanes did you fly?"

He mentioned casually, "Well, I flew fighters mostly—I logged a fair amount of time in the F-100 Super Sabre."

I perked up, wondering if this meek bookstore manager could really be cut from the same cloth as legendary test pilot Chuck Yeager, the first man to break the sound barrier. Eager to learn more, I asked Whitlow to detail his career for me. For the next half hour, Whitlow described a remarkable professional journey that included an assignment as a demonstration pilot with the United States Air Force Thunderbirds from 1957 through 1959.

You would have never known it looking at him there, sitting in the bookstore manager's chair.

Following our conversation, we became good friends. In addition to our meeting with some frequency during the next two decades, Whitlow took the time to write to me during extended periods when I was serving on temporary assignment overseas. His letters were encouraging, his advice always wise and on target. More than anything, I saw in Whitlow extraordinary humility. He devotes his time and energy to serving and enriching the lives of others—a higher purpose. He remains a wonderful role model.

Having the right kind of role model allows people to stiff-arm pride and emulate the character of someone farther along the journey toward more important things. As Norman Vincent Peale once said, "The more you lose yourself in something bigger than yourself, the more energy you will have."

Fortunately, culture-driven, people-centered organizations enjoy an abundance of such examples. Sur-

225

rounding yourself with people who are dedicated to a higher purpose is equivalent to marching into war with an army of trustworthy soldiers. *Going it alone is a mistake, regardless of how strong we imagine ourselves to be, because pride is more powerful than we give it credit for being.*

Sometimes pride creeps insidiously into our character, while other times it attacks with indiscriminate, overt force in a target-rich environment. In any case, culture-driven, people-centered organizations must foster humility while putting pride in its place.

FROM THE EXPRESS LANE

- ❀ Organizations must keep people focused on the future, not on the past.
- ❀ A focus on the future keeps people motivated to achieve whatever is necessary for sustained success.
- ❀ Organizations must keep people focused on the pursuit of excellence, not on the path to mediocrity.
- ❀ Organizations must keep people focused on the right kind of role models.
- ❀ Emulating the character of someone farther along the journey allows people to stiff-arm pride.

CONCLUSION

L EADERS HAVE SPENT far too much time focusing on fiscal resources and not enough time focusing on human resources. Long-term success is a result of putting more effort into building a positive, people-centered culture than poring over profit-and-loss statements.

Leaders need to challenge the existing business paradigm in a compelling manner by acting on the choice before them: continue to chase a broken price-profit model and suffer the consequences, or build a culture committed to people and servanthood, and discover the fulfillment found when team members see their work as a ministry. The choice leaders make will not only determine their organization's economic success and failure, but also determine the organization's long-term impact on humanity.

We need leaders actively participating in this movement. In his book *Leading Without Power*, Max De

Pree writes, "There is a harmony in relationships and a constructive conflict of ideas. There is a palpable unity as the people there implement their vision. There is a rhythm of innovation and renewal. There is a sense of urgency—movements are never casual." De Pree is right.

Time is of the essence—enriching the lives of human beings and the health of the communities in which they live depends on leaders bold enough to buck the trends. The business model in place today is a stagnant holdover from the Industrial Revolution. Worker bees place round pegs in round holes while management handles profit margins. It does not have to be this way.

The time is ripe for another workplace revolution, one driven by culture and synergy. A sustainable business must be about more than price and profit. An organization must be about people. It must instill a sense of higher purpose in employees so that providing quality service comes naturally. At a time when globalization has shrunk the world, leaders need to think big when it comes to motivating people in a highly competitive environment.

My hope is *Built to Serve* will become more than just another business book. As an active CEO, I understand the importance of the bottom line, but I also understand its limitations. In these pages, I have proposed an alternative: that culture, a manifestation of what we cultivate in people, drives the bottom line. It is a matter of conscious choice by leaders. Fortunately, some organizations understand the significance of the choices before them.

Certainly, the company I lead—one with a 90-year record of accomplishment in passionate customer service despite razor-thin profit margins in the supermarket industry—influences my thoughts and suggestions. However, other examples can be found in a wide array of industries—leaders and organizations spearheading the movement to shift the focus of the business marketplace from price and profit to a culture driving the business's economics.

229

I have shared some of those examples in this book, but many others exist. For example, Boston's Beth Israel Hospital, the first hospital in the world to publish a "Patient's Bill of Rights," and TDIndustries, a member of *Fortune* magazine's 100 Best Companies to Work for Hall of Fame, are radically different organizations, but they are similar in that they are creating their own culture-driven, people-centered bow waves.

I believe in human beings, and I believe human beings have a basic need to serve others. Work makes a difference in people's lives, and the most successful organizations are built around people who identify with their mission to the point that it becomes part of their very essence. Working in a culture defined by a higher purpose adds value to employees and those they serve, and creates a sea change in the way the business world operates.

Leaders need to liberate themselves from the denial-steeped past and embrace the dawn of a new era and a new culture—one that recognizes the economic power of an organization resides in people-first practices aimed at sustainability.

The bottom line is not about price and profit; it is about choice and culture.

The time is now.

CARRYOUT FOR LEADERS

❊ *Surrender your ego.* Surround yourself with talented people, and listen to what they have to say.

❊ *Preserve the culture.* The leader is the primary guardian of the culture.

❊ *Remain faithful to the values.* Do not compromise values, even when remaining faithful means doing things differently from the way everyone else does them.

❊ *Unleash the imagination.* Serve your team members, and they will give you their best.

❊ *Never stop talking about the purpose.* Make certain all team members connect what they do to the higher purpose of the organization.

❊ *Accept responsibility.* Leaders can delegate authority to their team members, but they can never delegate responsibility to their team members.

❊ *No job is unimportant.* Organizations are interdependent, and all team members must be working together to realize the potential of the team.

❊ *Do not compromise integrity.* Absolute truth is the best dividend any company can pay its stakeholders.

❊ *Execute as if your life depended on it.* The current business environment requires a sense of urgency like never before.

❊ *Have fun.* Higher productivity and greater guest satisfaction are the result of team members seeing their work as ministry.

AFTERWORD

F OR TOO MANY YEARS, leaders have passively accepted the myopic belief that the sole purpose of any business is to make a profit. In *Built to Serve*, Dan Sanders boldly challenges leaders to subscribe to a higher purpose, one that enriches the lives of others and the communities in which they live. Now that you have read this book, I hope you have the inspiration and courage to launch a servant leadership revolution within your own circle of influence.

Dan Sanders contends that an organization that places profits over people and growth over greatness is doomed for failure in the long run. Our research supports this claim. In a 2005 study, Scott Blanchard and Drea Zigarmi found that the vitality of an organization is directly related to employee passion and customer satisfaction. In other words, profit is the applause you get for taking care of your customers and creating a motivating environment for your people.

If leaders remain obsessed with spreadsheets and fail to recognize the importance of their people and their customers, their organizations will never realize their true potential. It does not have to be this way. Leaders interested in their organizations' long-term success should ask three simple questions:

1. What have we done for our customers?
2. What have we done for our people?
3. What have we done for our community?

Built to Serve calls for a profound shift in the philosophy and practice of business. Dan Sanders is uniquely qualified to deliver this message, as he draws upon his background as chief executive officer of United Supermarkets, an organization with a 90-year record of passionate customer service in an industry known for razor-thin margins. While most organizations measure success a quarter at a time, United measures success a quarter-century at a time. We can all learn a great deal from Dan's leadership and United's legacy.

It's time for leaders to understand that human beings find joy and fulfillment when they serve others.

Afterword

Leaders willing to leave the price-driven, profit-obsessed valley will find a far more satisfying view at the culture-inspired, people-centered summit. So, begin your journey today because the sooner you start, the sooner you will gain the loyalty of your customers, the trust of your employees, and the gratitude of your community.

Ken Blanchard
Chief Spiritual Officer
The Ken Blanchard Companies
Coauthor of *The One Minute Manager* and
    Leading at a Higher Level

INDEX

ABOUT THE CENTER FOR CORPORATE CULTURE

The Center for Corporate Culture became reality in 2007. It represents a new business standard, and it is designed to advocate an ongoing conversation about the importance of building a workplace culture engineered for maximum performance.

The seeds of The Center's evolution were planted in 2003, when The Dollins Group produced the first in a series of Ethical Leadership Conferences. The successful conferences have featured world-renowned speakers: Dr. Stephen R. Covey, Ken Blanchard, President George H. W. Bush, and General Norman Schwarzkopf. These brilliant thinkers engaged audiences and helped lay the foundation for The Center, which will continue that tradition of excellence by focusing on leadership, ethics, wellness and execution.

The Center's mission is to advocate an emerging twenty-first century business model at a time when business leaders face a bold new marketplace where competition is fierce, consumers are educated, and innovation is the chief currency. The Center is dedicated to helping CEOs and their teams focus on building a sustainable culture and enhancing their bottom line.

To learn more about The Center for Corporate Culture, visit www.thecenterforcorporateculture.com or address correspondence to 18333 Preston Road, Suite 220, Dallas, TX 75252.

ABOUT BUILT TO SERVE

Profits from *Built to Serve* will be donated to United We Care, a nonprofit organization created to assist United Supermarkets' team members and their families in extraordinary need. Representatives from throughout the company routinely meet to review requests for financial assistance. Approved requests are funded by voluntary contributions from team members throughout the organization. At the time of publication, United's 9,000 team members were voluntarily contributing more than $7,000 to the fund each week.

Thank you for taking the time to make *Built to Serve* a part of your life. Organizations, like churches, schools, and families, are made up of people, not buildings, playgrounds, or houses. Therefore, long-term success requires focusing on personal relationships. This seems to be a scary proposition for many leaders these days, but do not be paralyzed by fear. Be bold. Remember, people do not require perfect leaders—if they did, I would be among the first to be disqualified. I pray God will bless your efforts.

Most sincerely,

Dan